This book should be returned to any branch of the
Lancashire County Library on or before the date

Bark

‾ 4 AUG 2017

Lancashire County Library
Bowran Street
Preston PR1 2UX
www.lancashire.gov.uk/libraries

THE CANNY COLLECTOR

A COLLECTION OF QUOTES, HINTS, TIPS AND TRICKS TO INSPIRE AND HELP YOU TO BECOME A BETTER COLLECTOR

MARK HILL

ILLUSTRATED BY SIMON WATSON

This edition published in 2015 by New Holland Publishers Pty Ltd
London • Sydney • Auckland

The Chandlery, Unit 009 50 Westminster Bridge Road, London, SE1 7QY,
United Kingdom
1/66 Gibbes Street, Chatswood, NSW 2067, Australia
5/39 Woodside Ave, Northcote, Auckland 0627, New Zealand

www.newhollandpublishers.com

A record of this book is held at the British Library and the National Library of Australia.

ISBN 9781742578033

Managing Director: Fiona Schultz
Publisher: Alan Whiticker
Project Editor: Jessica McNamara
Production Director: Olga Dementiev
Printer: Toppan Leefung Printing Limited

10 9 8 7 6 5 4 3 2 1

Keep up with New Holla
www.facebook.com/New

Read Mark's blog at: www

CONTENTS

LEARNING

The more you learn, the more you realise there is to learn. One of the most exciting aspects of this world is that you never stop learning. As you become a better and more knowledgeable collector, try to find a balance. Don't forget to put back in what you took out and remember how you gained your knowledge.

DO SOME RESEARCH

Nearly all the greatest collectors in history were self-taught, and drew information from a range of sources from dealers to competitors, always with the objects as the main focus. The only other requirements are an unquenchable enthusiasm and hard work and a good dash of common sense.

Go out and buy a book. You'll redeem the cost of any book you buy many times over by reading and learning from them. The Canny Collector collects books on his or her collecting area, not just the objects alone.

Don't trust everything you read on the Internet, it is unedited, unchecked and anyone can post a 'fact'. Books are expensive to produce and harder to sell today, so they have to be edited well, and are typically written by, or checked with, experts.

When researching online, if you're not sure what keyword to search for, use resources such as Google Images. Type in words that relate to what you see in front of you. Think about how someone else might describe a piece. Once you've found it, and hopefully a maker or designer, double and triple check your findings to confirm them.

To develop and maintain your collector's eye, leaf through antiques price guides and auction catalogues – even if they're general and don't cover your chosen area. You'll be delighted by the information you pick up and link together as different things catch your eye.

None of the arts, be they fine or decorative, exist in a vacuum. Studying related fields such as architecture or social traditions opens up new levels of understanding to the Canny Collector.

Seek out original product catalogues and sales materials, as these often yield important discoveries, including all the variations of an object sold. Period magazines, such as *Ideal Home* and *House and Garden*, and trade publications, such as *Pottery Gazette and Glass Trade Review*, and VADS (www.vads.ac.uk) in the UK, or Carbone and Son or Raymor catalogues in the US, can be extremely helpful, particularly when it comes to competitors and how something was marketed and displayed at the time of sale or auction.

Accumulate knowledge, not only of the generic elements of leading styles such as Art Nouveau and Art Deco, but also of iconography and symbolism – the meaning of certain motifs or characters associated with that style.

When buying portraits, don't just consider the artist, think about the sitter too. A portrait of a famous or well-known sitter by an unknown artist will usually still be of interest. Similarly, a portrait of an unknown sitter by a famous artist will usually be of much less interest than a famous one, particularly if they were connected to the artist themselves, or the movement or period.

Before you invest, investigate.

J. PAUL GETTY, INDUSTRIALIST AND ART COLLECTOR

Know that attributions may change over time as newly unearthed facts reveal more about a piece – identifying marks, catalogues, and new first-hand reference materials, for example. Even the most traditional collecting areas – such as that of late 18th century, Liverpool porcelain – find their histories rewritten and challenged following revelations of one kind or another.

Keep abreast of what is coming up in the arts world. The sale of a major collection, the publication of a catalogue raisonné, or the opening of a public exhibition often causes a sharp rise in interest, demand and value.

Research every new piece when you get it home. Chances are, it will take you down an interesting path to understanding its unique story. Along the way, you'll pick up all sorts of new information.

If you have an object from a relative and have already learnt about its history and story, type it up and keep it with the piece, even if you have no proof of what you have been told. It may be that your great grandmother was a lady in waiting to Queen Victoria, who gave her the locket you now hold, or the cigarette case you received previously belonged to your grandfather, who kept it in his pocket at Somme, and the dent is where it saved his life by deflecting a bullet. Otherwise its history dies with you.

Although it's an impressive feat to correctly identify, date and value a piece, the Canny Collector will assess and enjoy all the other qualities and stories an object presents.

GET OUT AND ABOUT

Aim to visit the auctions of entire collections and buy catalogues. It's fun to spot the themes and inspirations that run through the often wildly diverse objects that collectors buy.

Visit vetted fairs before starting out with a collection, so that you can learn accurate information. You want to be able to trust what's on the ticket.

Go to museums to see the best and to observe how the pieces relate to each other and fit into the context of the age. You'd be surprised at what some museums hold, for example, London's Victoria and Albert Museum has a ceramics display that includes designs right up to today.

Whenever you visit a museum, find out what its newest acquisitions are. Museum curators are often an incredibly helpful source of knowledge. A deep understanding of a given area is critical to this job and very useful to the Canny Collector.

HANDLE THE GOODS

Always aim to handle as much as you can. This allows you to learn first-hand about colour, weight, marks and the general feel of an object. If done repeatedly, all these things will stick in your mind. So it's just as important to handle as many fakes or reproductions as you can, too.

Nobody can give you advice after you've been collecting for a while. If you don't enjoy making your own decisions, you're never going to be much of a collector anyway.

CHARLES SAATCHI, ADVERTISING GURU AND ART COLLECTOR

Take time every now and again to pick up and examine pieces
that are deemed to be bad or poor quality.
This will quickly refresh your mind as to why
they are described as such.

Large fairs, antiques centres and auction views offer
an opportunity to handle a variety of pieces.
Auction views are usually held for a day or so before
an auction happens. Make good use of the expert staff
on hand if you have any questions.

The Canny Collector uses all five senses available, not just sight
and feel. The sound made by tapping something,
the feel of a surface, the smell of an old textile,
and the taste of a fine wine to top it all off!

When looking at something for the first time, stand back and
assess the obvious first – size, shape, proportions, balance,
colours and materials. Then examine the finer details before
drawing your final thoughts together.

DEVELOP YOUR EYE

The all-important 'good eye' is supported by a great visual
memory and in-depth knowledge, but is independent enough
to make fresh and original decisions and judgements.

Whether at a fair, gallery, or museum,
the Canny Collector looks at an object
before looking at its label. Once you've formed
your judgement, check it against the label
and feel satisfied because you got it right,
or because you've learned something new.

When you're starting out, look at the best pieces. Not only are they more exciting and fulfilling to look at, but they sum up the style of a given period. They are also likely to be key pieces that other designers and makers were inspired by. You'll learn a good deal about quality and will be able to identify key themes and motifs in objects in the future.

INSIDER KNOWLEDGE

Make friends with a dealer and an auction house specialist. Buy from them and sell with them. The majority are keen enthusiasts with a deep specialist knowledge that they'll be happy to share with you in the course of doing business. Like any relationship, it's about balance.

Don't play dealers or experts off against one another, as this only causes antagonism. The art and antiques world is surprisingly small and people talk, even if they dislike each other. You'll only build up a bad reputation for yourself.

Don't be scared of the lingo. Learn it and use it just as you'd learn words and phrases on a foreign holiday. There's a strangely enjoyable, esoteric pleasure to be gained from using the right words to describe something. It's often quicker, too, as many features can only be described easily by using specialist phrases.

Meet as many object makers or designers as you can. Their stories can open up new avenues of understanding that only they have access to. They can also help you identify and explain why items are rarities.

My father is an engineer. He taught me that, in order to appreciate an item fully, you have to understand how it was made. Pieces that are complex, time-consuming to make, or are made from expensive materials are likely to be of interest in today's market.

Understanding the techniques used to make an item allows you to understand how a maker has mastered those techniques and his chosen material, and to judge whether or not they have united them successfully with design.

Don't forget the social side of collecting. It's not just a solitary occupation. Join a club or society, attend auctions, and go to fairs. You'll learn plenty by swapping information with other collectors and enthusiasts. You'll also have an opportunity to handle, and perhaps even buy, pieces you may not see otherwise.

If invited to another collector's home you should go, even if you're not interested in his or her collection. You'll find out all sorts of things that you can apply to your own collection or collecting habits, and you will find the experience surprisingly enjoyable.

WHAT TO COLLECT?

Consider items that appeal to a wide range of collectors. An Edwardian postcard of a lady tennis player will appeal to postcard collectors, tennis memorabilia collectors, and collectors interested in the history of women's rights, or fashion. A larger audience and increased competition will push the price of an object higher.

Since the 18th century, wealthy industrialists, financiers and oligarchs have set the high-end collecting trends and everyone else has followed as best they can. During the 18th century, British aristocrats pillaged Italy for classical Roman antiquities (or copies of them) for their newly built Palladian mansions. In the early 20th century Henry Clay Frick and J. Paul Getty collected 'gilt-edged' French rococo and 'Louis-style' pieces. More recently, Roman Abramovich is known for collecting contemporary and modern art for his palatial minimalist interiors. What will the next generation collect?

The Canny Collector goes for quality over quantity. One truly great quality piece in near-mint condition will always be a better bet for the future than, say, five 'good-quality' pieces in average or poor condition.

Early memorabilia, or memorabilia produced for the biggest names or events usually attracts the highest prices. However, it can pay to look out for memorabilia from smaller names or events. Typically, far fewer pieces will have been produced and surprisingly high prices may be paid by keen and completely dedicated collectors.

The earliest examples of most objects will always be of interest (but not necessarily great value) to a collector.

Stamps and coins are perhaps two of the widest and longest collected objects. In many cases, they've also proved to be reliably solid investments. One is intrinsically valuable (most coins are made from precious metals) while the other is not. Devotion to both can start early and become ingrained in a personality. Even though budgets differ, both can be (and are) collected by individuals ranging from school children to royalty, and seem to be largely resistant to the changing vagaries of fashion.

A signature – such as that of an author in a book they wrote, or of a celebrity on a photograph of themself – usually adds value to a piece. If it's dedicated to someone, that value is often reduced, as the piece is only of interest to that person

I firmly believe that almost anyone can become a collector, and that he or she can start collecting at almost any period of life. One need not be an expert or have large amounts of money to start ...

J. PAUL GETTY, INDUSTRIALIST AND ART COLLECTOR

COLLECTIONS TO VISIT

Even if you don't have the means to immortalize your own collection for eternity, aim to visit those of collectors who have or did. You'll find them inspirational as well as educational, even if they're outside your usual collecting area. Most of the collections in this list were founded or built by a single collector, and are all particularly inspirational in their own ways. This is by no means a comprehensive list, and you won't find the world's major museums here, as you should know about those already. Many museums, like the British Museum in London and the Smithsonian in Washington, D.C., contain a number of collections donated by the people that built them.

BRITISH ISLES
Bowes Museum, Barnard Castle, Co. Durham, thebowesmuseum.org.uk
Burrell Collection, Glasgow, Scotland, glasgowlife.org.uk
Dennis Severs House, London, dennissevershouse.co.uk
Duke Humfrey's Library, Bodleian Library, Oxford, bodleian.ox.ac.uk
The Fan Museum, London, thefanmuseum.org.uk
Haworth Art Gallery, Accrington, Lancashire, hyndburnbc.gov.uk/hag
Horniman Museum, London, horniman.ac.uk
House on the Hill Toy Museum, Stansted, Essex, stanstedtoymuseum.com
The Hunt Museum, Limerick, Ireland, huntmuseum.com
Kettle's Yard, Cambridge, kettlesyard.co.uk
King's Library, British Museum, London, britishmuseum.org
Lady Lever Art Gallery, Port Sunlight, liverpoolmuseums.org.uk/ladylever
Museum of Brands, London, museumofbrands.com
Pitt Rivers Museum, Oxford, prm.ox.ac.uk
Powell Cotton Museum, Birchington, Kent, quexpark.co.uk
Sainsbury Centre for Visual Arts, Norwich, Norfolk, scva.org.uk
Sir John Soane Museum, London, soane.org
Vintage Radio and Television Museum, London, bvwtm.org.uk
Wallace Collection, London, wallacecollection.org

USA
The Barnes Collection, Philadelphia, Pennsylvania, barnesfoundation.org
The Frick Collection, Manhattan, New York, frick.org
The Gardner Museum, Boston, Massachusetts, gardnermuseum.org
The Getty Villa and Museum, Los Angeles, California, getty.edu
The Morgan Library and Museum, Manhattan, New York, themorgan.org
The Morse Museum, Winter Park, Florida, morsemuseum.org
The Phillips Collection, Washington, D.C., phillipscolletion.org
The Ringling Collection, Sarasota, Florida, ringling.org
The Rosenbach Museum and Library, Philadelphia, rosenbach.org
Winterthur Museum and Gallery, Winterthur, Delaware, winterthur.org

OTHER COUNTRIES
Argentina - National Museum of Decorative Arts, Buenos Aires, mnad.org
France - Musée Cernuschi, Paris, cernuschi.paris.fr
France - Musée des Arts Forains, Paris, arts.forains.com
France - Musée de la Musique Mécanique, Les Gets, musicmecalesgets.org
France - Musée des Poupées, Josellin, museedepoupees.fr
France - Musée Jacquemart-André, Paris, musee-jacquemart-andre.com
Germany - Berggruen Collection, Berlin, skb.museum
Germany - Buchstaben Museum, Berlin, buchstabenmuseum.de
Germany - Green Vault (Grünes Gewölbe), Dresden, skd.museum
Germany - Passau Glass Museum, Passau, glasmuseum.de
Germany - The Zwinger, numerous collections, Dresden, skd.museum
Italy - Borghese Gallery, Rome, galleriaborghese.it
Italy - Museo Nazionale dell'Automobile, Turin, museoauto.it
Italy - Palazzo and Villa Doria Pamphilj, Rome and Genoa, dopart.it
Netherlands - Kröller-Müller Museum, Otterlo, kmm.nl
Poland - Museum Czartoryski, Cracow, muzeum-czartoryskich.krakow.pl
Poland - Przypkowskich w. Jedrzejowie, Jedrzejów, muzeum.jedrzejow.pl
Portugal - Museu Calouste Gulbenkian, Lisbon, museu.gulbenkian.pt
Portugal - Museu do Brinquedo, Sintra, museu-do-brinquedo.pt
Spain - Museo Cerralbo, Madrid, en.museocerralbo.mcu.es
Spain - Thyssen-Bornemisza Collection, Madrid, museothyssen.org
Sweden - Hallwylska Museum, Stockholm, hallwylskamuseet.se

or someone with the same name. Conversely, if the person it's dedicated to is famous or connected to the life or work of the person who signed it, that may increase the value dramatically. Drawings or extra personal information also add value.

The contents of a letter or document are of vital importance to its desirability and value. If some aspect of the writer's personality is revealed, or if the text relates to an important, famous or infamous part of their life, then so much the better. Simple thank-you letters, especially those sent out on an official basis, are usually of considerably less interest or value.

The best private collections of seemingly unrelated objects, are often the best, as they're united by the collector's passion, soul, vision, personality and knowledge – qualities that are allowed to shine through.

The worst collections are often those built using an open chequebook, where a 'collector' hands over cash and responsibility to a dealer or interior designer.

An interesting provenance can more than double the value of a piece, particularly if it relates to a famous personality, house, or collection.

Bragging rights aside, second or third rate pieces by first-tier artists or makers usually perform worse than first-rate pieces by second or third tier artists or makers.

People living in politically or economically unstable countries often collect intrinsically valuable, portable items that have value across the world – diamonds, jewellery or objects made from precious metals.

There are plenty of things to collect in these financially tight and insecure times. Examples include packaging, such as crisp packets or sugar packets and promotional items, such as business cards or postcards from companies you use or visit. These things typically represent the styles and desires of the day and collections of them show how such things change quickly over time to attract attention. By-products from living an early 21st century life such as newspapers, magazines, and even wallpaper will do the same.

Don't feel discouraged from collecting everyday, practical, household items from the past. They may not be high art, but the stories they tell about our history and how we used to live are an invaluable insight to our past.

We regard Clarice Cliff, English ceramics designer, as comparatively modern and 'recent'. However, her best ceramics were made over 80 years ago. It's interesting to think that, when our grandparents were building their collections, the early-19th century porcelain figurines and ceramics that formed the core of many collections were of a similar age.

It may seem too recent, but consider collecting Postmodern pieces from the 1980s. This decade is as distant today as the 1930s were when the Canny Collectors of the 1960s began acquiring Art Deco objects. Both styles share some similarities, and have a similarly bold and easily identifiable look.

Consider collecting work made by the best and most respected artists and craftsmen working today, as much of it will be sought after tomorrow.

Being a Canny Collector is ten per cent inspiration, thirty per cent luck, and sixty per cent perspiration.

THE AUTHOR

Fields that are particularly good for this include furniture, jewellery, studio ceramics and studio glass.

Beauty really is in the eye of the beholder. One man's trash is almost certainly another man's treasure. This is obvious to anyone who has sat and watched how people move through a museum or art gallery.

As an area becomes more popular and prices rise, many collectors move on to other areas. If you can't afford to collect something, you swiftly find something else. Collectors must collect – it's what we do.

Don't buy because of a name alone. The work should have pleasing and aesthetic qualities, and be indicative of the artist or maker's style.

Always look at boxes or suitcases of old photographs, even if they seem like holiday snaps or memories of everyday life at first. Look closer - some can be fascinating records of how we used to live. At one extreme, in 2009, an archive of over 150,000 photographs by an unknown nanny called Vivian Maier was discovered at a storage centre auction. Depicting changing everyday street life across the second half of the 20th century, it's now considered a highly important and valuable archive of American social history. Although this may be a unique find, even single photos can be of interest, for example if they show themes such as trades, factory life, or attitudes to race, gender or sexuality. Usually affordable, some may simply make you smile or laugh!

Everything I buy is vintage and smells funny.
Maybe that's why I don't have a boyfriend.

LUCY LIU, HOLLYWOOD ACTRESS

CONSIDER AVAILABILITY

Like most markets, the value of an antique or collectable is
based on supply and demand. If supply drops, or is limited,
and demand increases, the value rises. If something is
commonly found or is unfashionable
or undesirable, its value will usually be low.
The Canny Collector is able to identify those areas
that are about to return to desirability and fashion.

THE INFLUENCE OF FASHION

Consider the 'Thirty Year Rule'. Pieces tend to spend 30 years
in fashion, 30 years out of fashion, and 30 years in again. Most
people consider things that their parents owned as awful and
things that their grandparents owned as cool.

We often date pieces to a few years, or within
a small time period as a guideline. Fashion trends used
to change far slower than they do today.
As such, one style could have been made much
later than initially thought.

Look out for artists, designers and makers who started
popular trends, or grew to dominate them. Even if the look
is out of fashion today, that may change in the future. Pieces
by such people have a place in history and will always be
important to someone.

Fashion may influence a change in demand for furniture, but
there are always other, more practical considerations, too.
Newly built houses tend to have smaller rooms, which means
smaller furniture is more desirable. Pieces that were practical
one hundred years ago may be less so today. For example,
most bureaus cannot accommodate a desktop computer
or laptop with its associated cables. Prices of such pieces
generally plummet as a result.

For some reason, a number of great makers or designers are routinely passed over by the collecting community. This won't happen forever, however, and the few Canny Collectors who are buying up their work will soon be rewarded for their prescience and faith. Examples from the 20th century include sculptures by Brian Willsher and ceramics designed by John Clappison for Hornsea.

The past decade has seen a downturn in the value of many traditional antiques. Sadly, that's unlikely to change until there's a sea-change in interior design trends. Most families inheriting such pieces tend to find them unfashionable and put them up for sale. The result reflects the rule of supply and demand: the supply is increasing and demand is not growing as quickly.

Many people think that the collecting of TV, film, cartoon and related memorabilia is a new fad. Newspapers report that it was healthy and strong in the early 1970s, attracting fans such as the actor Dustin Hoffman. Despite it being tagged 'kitsch' at the time, this makes it a firmly established market.

YOUR JOURNEY

Collecting is made up of a series of journeys that begin with the smallest step – the purchase of the first piece. What follows may lead you through history or to other countries; it may introduce you to alternative societies and systems of belief. Even collectors who are determined to specialise will be led down different byways and detours.

In my opinion, an individual without any love of the arts cannot be considered completely civilized.

J. PAUL GETTY, INDUSTRIALIST AND ART COLLECTOR

MARKS, DATING AND IDENTIFICATION

Marks on the base of a ceramic piece can be instantly helpful:

• A piece bearing only a country name (such as 'England') usually dates from 1891–1921.

• 'Made in' followed by the name of a country in English indicates the piece was made after 1921. There are a few exceptions, such as Wedgwood, who may have used this style from c.1908, and 'Made in Germany', which can date from after 1887, due to the 1887 Merchandise Act.

• 'Limited' or 'Ltd' after the name of a company was used after 1861.

• A mark incorporating a coat of arms dates from after c.1800.

• 'Royal' in a name indicates a piece was made no earlier than the second half of the 19th century, but most likely dates from later.

• 'Bone China' (possibly with the addition of 'Fine' and/or 'English') indicates a piece dates from the 20th or 21st century.

• Marks incorporating printed pattern names indicate a piece was made after c.1810.

'D.R.G.M.' stands for 'Deutsches Reichsgebrauchsmuster', which indicates the design or function was registered in Germany and was produced from 1891–1952. After 1952, the style changed to 'D.B.G.M.' (Deutsches Bundesgebrauchsmuster) or 'Gebrauchsmuster'. 'D.R.P.' or (less common) 'D.R.' stands for 'Deutsches Reichspatent', which was introduced in 1877. 'Ges. Gesch.' is an abbreviated form of 'Gesetzlich Geschützt', which indicates that the piece was legally protected in Germany. All were mainly used after c.1900.

'West Germany' or 'W.Germany' or 'F.R.G.' indicates a piece was produced there from 1949–1990. 'G.D.R.', 'D.D.R.' (Deutsche Demokratische Republik), 'V.E.B.' (Volkseigener Betrieb), or 'P.G.H.' indicates a piece was made in East Germany during the same period.

Pieces marked 'Nippon' date from around 1891–1921. If they are marked 'Japan', they date from around 1921–41, and if they are marked 'Made in Occupied Japan', they date from 1945 to April 1952.

Pieces marked 'Czechoslovakia' date from 1918–c.1995 after which 'Czech Republic' was used. 'Čechoslovakia' indicates a piece was made 1918–20, before a revision to the McKinley Tariff Act.

Patent and registered numbers (prefixed 'Rd. No.', 'Registered' or 'Rd.') are useful in finding out when a piece was designed and first made. If the design was successful, it could have been made for many years after. US patents and, if registered before 1919, British patents expired after 14 years. The term was then 17 years before becoming the standard 20 years in 1995.

In Britain, a motif of a diamond with a circle on top was used for design registrations from 1842–1888. Some of the numbers inside the diamond's segments indicate the date of the registration of the design. Registration numbers, typically prefixed 'Reg'd No.' were used from 1884–1980. In the US, utility patent numbers were introduced in 1836 and design patent numbers in 1843.

The words 'Brevet' or 'Breveté' indicate a French patent, and 'Déposé' indicates a French registered design or trademark depending on the word before it. The initials 'S.G.D.G.' stand for 'Sans Garantie du Gouvernement' which means 'Patented Without State Guarantee'. All date from after 1844, but were mainly used after c.1900.

'Brevetti' is an Italian patent mark similar to 'Brevet' in France, above, and 'Eneret' is the Danish equivalent.

'Pat. Pend.' indicates that a patent had been filed, but not yet granted. Similar terms include 'Patent Applied For' and 'Patent Pending'.

The word 'Copyright' was only used after 1858, but was mainly used in the 20th century. The © symbol was introduced in the US in 1909.

'Trademark' was used after 1862 in Great Britain, and after 1867 in the US.

Treat your relationship with collecting like a relationship with money. It's great to have everything organised and looked after, but don't become obsessed. Just as you wouldn't let money become an obstacle to a personal relationship, don't allow your collecting to get in the way, either.

Hang on to your first mistake, if you can, to remind yourself that enthusiasm needs to be restrained by knowledge and to demonstrate how far you have come (and still have to go).

Don't over analyse the reasons behind why you collect. It's a little like a joke – when you try to work out why it's funny it ceases to be so. It's the same with collecting, so just enjoy doing it and enjoy getting better at it.

Over the past few years, the word 'antique' has almost become derided and despised. Instead, the word 'vintage' has replaced it and attracted a younger audience of new collectors. Although the 'vintage' market primarily involves fashion and 20th century objects, the eccentric and individual mix that makes it up includes antiques too. 'Retro' pieces are different and usually date from the 1950s–70s. It's likely that 'vintage' and 'retro' will continue to be important.

Many say that collecting is dead because young people are not interested in it, while those who are, only pay small amounts of money, and infrequently at that. But most young people are rightly more concerned about paying the mortgage, bills and supporting a family than buying antiques. As they get older and amounts of disposable income grow, however, their current interest in 'vintage' and 'retro' should mature and develop. Don't lose heart and think positively. The interest is there, it's just that the money and time aren't – yet.

Objects and works of art do not tell lies. They're inanimate objects. The descriptions and labels we apply to them can be wrong or misleading. We simply need to learn and understand how to read and see what's in front of us.

If you collect, it's with you for life. In the 1960s, a survey found that 80 per cent of boys and 66 per cent of girls collected something, and the majority continued collecting later in life. Don't fight it, enjoy it!

Fads and changing fashions can cause sharp rises in price, but many are temporary. However, quality and style endure. In 1964, an Art Deco bronze and ivory figure by Demetre Chiparus was sold by a theatrical prop hire company for £8. In 1972, around the time when the Art Deco style began to be widely reappraised and taken seriously, another fetched nearly £200 at auction at Phillips. In 1976, another at Sotheby's fetched £5,200. Today, depending on the model, the price could exceed £100,000.

To me, works of art are all vividly alive. They are the embodiment of whoever created them – a mirror of their creator's hopes, dreams and frustrations. They have led eventful lives – pampered by the aristocracy and pillaged by revolution, courted with ardour and cold-bloodedly abandoned. They have been honoured by drawing rooms and humbled by attics. So many worlds in their life-span, yet all were transitory. Their worlds have long since disintegrated, yet they live on – and, for the most part, they are as beautiful as ever.

ETHEL LE VANE, AUTHOR

BUYING

We can't resist it, it's the lifeblood activity of collecting. It's easy to spend money, but harder to buy well. But always remember, it's the things you don't buy that you will regret the most.

SOUND ADVICE

Go to an antiques fair at the start and at the finish. At the start, you'll see the most desirable and best pieces, which will sell during the course of the fair. At the end you'll discover what didn't sell and you may be able to secure a piece you like (if it's still there) for less.

If you can't afford a painting, see if the artist produces prints. Limited editions often prove to be good investments.

Taking an object of average quality and value out of a high-end saleroom can pay. By placing it in a lower-end sale in a general or provincial auction house, it can become, by comparison, a 'top lot' and may attract more attention and bids. The buyer's premium might also be less there, again encouraging bidding.

The greatest art and work of tomorrow often remains unsold when it is first offered for sale. This is often because they challenge what is accepted at the time and collectors and society have to catch up with them. Just think of Vincent van Gogh.

If you can't decide whether to buy a piece, think of preparing and eating breakfast tomorrow morning. If you think you'll remember the item and wish you'd bought it, reach for your cash.

Your collection is a living thing – like a plant. It will grow through buying and will need cutting back through selling. It'll also change direction from time to time.

Don't feel bad if your collection is criticised
for having no focus – the focus is you and your
taste and life, as you've built it all up.

STARTING OUT

Do your research first. You wouldn't buy
stocks or shares without doing research
into the company, would you?

In order to be successful, you have to learn as much as
you can about a subject and anything that crosses into it.

Investigate import and export laws in different
countries. They vary, and you don't want to have to pay
large additional taxes or import duties or, worse, not be
able to take your newly found treasure home with you.

Always make sure that you have a 'holy grail'
otherwise the thrill goes out of the hunt.

BUYING AT AUCTION

Set yourself a limit before going into an auction
room, and don't exceed it! If you're worried about
over-spending on an online auction site like eBay,
try using sniping software, which places a bid as late
as possible. You'll need to enter your top bid into the
system, and it will then be executed automatically.
You can always modify it before the auction ends if you
wish. This way you won't get carried away in the last
few minutes of an auction.

*I've started collecting taxidermy. I've got a red squirrel
called Steve. I made sure he came with certificates so
we know he wasn't just killed for stuffing.*

ARTHUR DARVILL, ACTOR

Don't worry that you'll make a bid accidentally by scratching your nose or head. That's a myth. If you're not already known to the auctioneer, you may even have to say something to attract his or her attention, or he or she may ask you to confirm that you are bidding. To carry on bidding, either wave your paddle, or nod clearly whilst looking at the auctioneer. When you've reached your maximum price and finished bidding, either firmly look away or shake your head when the auctioneer looks at you to offer you the next bid. He or she may ask you if you are sure, but will then move on.

Auctions generally move up in increments of 10 per cent, depending on the value of the piece, so £5s, £10s, £20s, £50s, £100s, £1000s. Your bid will be the next increment up from the one announced, and you needn't shout out your bid. The auctioneer will control the increments and the bidding, so it's impolite to keep shouting out prices unless you want to pay considerably more than the active bid.

Halving a bid (by shouting out an offer of, say £90, when the current bid is £80 and the next bid would be £100) is tricky, but it can work to achieve an economical lot price, or to hit someone's maximum bid if you're bidding on their behalf. Only do it once when you absolutely have to, and make sure it's worthwhile in terms of value. You'll irritate an auctioneer and the other bidders if you repeatedly shout out a halved bid, especially if you are working at a level under a few hundred pounds.

If the auctioneer seems to be taking bids from a non-existent person, don't be alarmed. To get, and keep, the bidding going, the auctioneer often opens with a price below the 'reserve' price of the item. The reserve price is the lowest price the seller is prepared to accept. All the auctioneer is doing is bouncing bids 'off the wall' to reach the reserve price so that he or she can sell it, particularly if there is only one bidder, or no bidder at all.

'The book' is a term used to describe a list of bids left by people who cannot attend the auction. Known as commission bids, these are executed on the day of the sale by the auctioneer (who will often point at his desk when executing one) or a member of staff seated nearby. They are confidential and will be executed as low as possible.

Don't forget to factor 'buyer's premium' into your limit. This is the commission an auction house adds on to the hammer price (the price a lot sells for). Although it can be as low as 10 per cent, it can also be as high as 30 per cent. National, regional or state taxes may also apply.

Pay close attention to the catalogue. The presence of a symbol near the pre-sale estimate, lot number, or description may indicate that these taxes are applied to the hammer price as well as the buyer's premium. Ignore or disregard them at your peril!

Do not get involved in a 'ring'. This is an illegal practice where a group of people – often dealers – group together and choose what they want to buy. The members of the ring will not bid against each other, or only one will buy on behalf of the ring, thereby keeping the price low. Sometimes, although it is very rare, a ring will bid against other bidders to inflate the price greatly and discourage them from bidding again.

Take a tape measure when looking at furniture, as it can be difficult to get a feeling for how the piece will fit into your home in terms of size, particularly in a typically cavernous auction house. Also consider the size of access points such as doors, or even windows.

People always say "Congratulations". When you're the successful bidder, it means you're willing to spend more than anyone else. I'm not sure if that's congratulations or condolences.

ELI BROAD, BUSINESS TYCOON AND PHILANTHROPIST

If you can't go to view a piece yourself, ask the auction house for a verbal or written condition report. Ask for all the details you need in order to make a decision. If you're still unsure, ask for photographs to be emailed.

Always check out general sales if you can. You may spot something that the auction house cataloguer hasn't spotted, or has not identified or described correctly – especially in a box lot. In these days of illustrated online catalogues, these sales are one of the last places it's possible to spot a 'sleeper'.

Always check saleroom announcements in case there have been changes to the lots you are interested in. Lots are sometimes withdrawn from sale at the last minute, and you won't want to be waiting for a non-existent lot!

Leave enough time to register for a bidding number before your lot comes up for sale. Call the auction house to find out approximately when your lot may come up. Most auctioneers sell over 100 lots per hour.

Always tear up, hand in, or take your numbered bidding paddle with you when you leave, so that it isn't used by someone else.

Although auctioneers may proceed briskly through an auction at 80–120 lots per hour, the advent of online bidding direct into salerooms has slowed the pace. Sometimes, particularly if online activity is strong, the rate can slow to 30–40 lots per hour. Another result is that previous packed-out salerooms are now often nearly deserted. An empty auction room doesn't mean you'll get a bargain!

Collecting is my joy, it gives me great satisfaction.

URSULA ANDRESS, ACTRESS

Although they may seem like the preserve of the professional dealer or experienced collector, auction houses are acting increasingly like dealers or other retail outlets, and are keen to encourage as many people through the door as possible. Fully illustrated catalogues like magazines, coffee shops, lectures and 'At Home' style interior-led auctions are typical. This often causes friction with dealers, who don't appreciate their territory being encroached upon. It's also very different from the 1970s and before, when catalogues rarely had images, only had the most basic descriptions – and gave no indication at all of what one may have to pay!

Theoretically, at auction, the sky's the limit for a price if two people are determined to own something. But the one type of sale where unusually high prices across the board are seen more frequently are grand country house auctions. As well as often being desirably 'fresh to the market', and maybe in totally original condition, people will often pay considerably over the odds to own a piece from their local country pile, or maybe one that they visited. Don't expect a bargain!

Although architectural salvage and antiques can often appear more affordable at auctions, don't forget to factor in transport (and even restoration) costs for purchases that can be heavy, cumbersome, very large or made up of many parts. Many auction houses will also want purchases collected within days, otherwise storage charges apply. Because some objects, such as tiles, are also usually sold in large quantities, you may also find that you have to buy much more than you need!

My room is like an antiques shop, full of junk and weird stuff. There's a big sword in there. And a taxidermy bird and a couple of bird cages. And a lot of newspaper cuttings ...

FLORENCE WELCH, SINGER, FLORENCE AND THE MACHINE

BUYING OUT IN THE OPEN

If you're going to a car boot sale, flea market, or antiques or collectors fair, take plenty of cash. Most dealers don't take credit or debit cards and may be reluctant to accept a cheque. You may also be able to negotiate a better price with cash!

If you're interested in something at a fair, pick it up, or at least place your hand on it. There's an unwritten rule that the person touching an item has a claim and first refusal on buying it.

If you're interested in a number of items, group them together but don't show any special interest in one item. This can be useful if you've spotted a real bargain and want to draw any potential interest or attention away from it.

It's more fun to shop with someone else, but make sure they don't collect the same things as you. Always hand something you're interested in buying to your shopping partner so that they can check it for damage or problems. You might have missed some in the excitement!

DEALING WITH DEALERS

The greatest dealers are those who recognize a great artist or 'sleeping' area and put their money where their vision is. Many appear to border on insane in doing so!

Always ask the seller. No question is too stupid if politely and genuinely put. Shop around, too. You do the same when buying a flat-screen TV or washing machine and buying an antique or vintage piece is no different.

Most dealers are prepared to haggle, but do so politely and respectfully, and only expect a 10 per cent discount if you're paying with cash.

Remember that dealers have mortgages,
travel and other overheads, and need to eat.
Plus they work extremely hard to find the piece
that you're about to buy!

Tailor your language to match the occasion when
haggling, but always be friendly, relaxed and open
about what you can or want to pay. Although being
casual will work fine in open-air markets, you'll need
a different vocabulary and set of negotiation skills
in a smart fair or city centre gallery.

When haggling, don't just point out what's wrong with
something. You'll only irritate the dealer and, if it's so bad,
why do you want to buy it? If there are faults, point them
out, but negotiate in other ways, such as stating what you
can afford to pay and seeing what happens next.

General dealers at a fair can make excellent sport.
Although they may be very knowledgeable about one or
two areas, if they sell a broad spectrum of things, it's likely
their eye for quality and a good deal will have missed a
rarity. Here, the specialist, niche collector can really win.

The best, and most successful, dealers buy in times of a
recession, investing in stock at lower prices while others
cut back. It also allows lucky collectors, who may not be
so seriously affected economically, to buy things they
may otherwise be unable to afford.

CHARITY SHOPS

Check, check and check again. Most are aware of the
value of things due to TV and the Internet and there's
probably a reason why someone gave it to a charity shop.

Don't haggle in a charity shop. Remember where your money
is going, and who it is going to help. If you're lucky enough to
find a real bargain, consider making an extra donation.

Charity shops in wealthy areas are always worth visiting, and don't forget to check out the clothes and accessories such as handbags and belts if you collect fashion. Even holiday souvenirs from previous decades can fetch good money. A Mdina Glass 'Fish' vase bought as a souvenir on Malta in the early 1970s can fetch over £1,000 today.

BUYING ONLINE

If you have a spare hour to kill, browse through broad categories on eBay and other online auction sites. Quite often, sellers don't know what an item is, or when, where, or by whom it was made. Alternatively search under general terms, such as 'huge glass vase' or 'blue bowl'.

Search eBay sites in other countries, such as Canada, Australia, Germany and France, particularly if the objects you collect were made there or exported there in large quantities. Don't forget to translate your usual search terms into the correct language.

Search online under common misspellings of names, as you may find a bargain. An obvious example is 'Wedgewood', but also consider how someone may spell a name phonetically.

Set up a separate email account for your Paypal, eBay and other payment and online auction subscriptions. That way you'll be able to avoid phishing and other scams, and track how that email address is used by people you buy from or sell to.

I don't think any collector knows his true motivation.

ROBERT MAPPLETHORPE, PHOTOGRAPHER

KNOW WHAT YOU'RE BUYING

The art and antiques world, particularly fine art auctioneers use different wording to describe a piece in terms of who made it, how it is signed and when it was made. Don't be dazzled by famous names, but read the wording carefully. Most of the following conventions are applied to flat art, such as paintings or drawings, but may also be applied to pieces in other media. Always read the entire description and, if in doubt, ask or consult the auction house's or dealer's catalogue or website for clarification.

'Attributed to...'
In their opinion, this is a work by the artist or maker whose name follows the term, in whole or in part.

'After...'
In their opinion, a copy of a work by the artist or maker, produced at any date after the original.

'Follower of...'
In their opinion a work produced in the style of the artist or maker, but not necessarily by a pupil of that artist.

'Circle of...'
In their opinion a work made during the period the artist or maker was alive, and showing his or her influence.

'Manner of...'
In their opinion a work produced in the artist's or maker's style, but produced by someone else at a later date.

'Studio of...' or 'Workshop of...'
In their opinion, a work produced in the studio or workshop of the artist or maker, possibly under his or her supervision.

'In the ... style' or '... style'
Although the piece is in, for example the Art Deco style, in their opinion it was not made during that period, and was made later.

'Style of...' or '...pattern'
In their opinion, a copy or imitation of a piece by the artist or maker.

'Signed...', 'Dated...', Inscribed...',
In their opinion, the work has been signed, dated or inscribed by the artist or maker. If a question mark follows, this indicates doubt on behalf of the specialist who catalogued it. You will need to satisfy yourself as to whether the signature, date or inscription is authentic or not before bidding.

'With signature...', 'With inscription', 'Inscribed...', 'Bears signature...'
In their opinion, the signature or inscription may be of the artist or maker, but was applied by someone else.

'Dated...'
The work bears a date and, in their opinion, the work was produced at the date that follows.

'Bears date...'
The work bears a date but, in their opinion, the piece may not have been made at the date that follows.

Names only
If the full name of the artist or maker appears on its own at the start of the description, the work being described is by that artist. Sometimes only an artist's or maker's surname is used. This usually indicates that the piece is a copy of their work, or is a work by another maker or artist in their style. The rest of the description should verify this.

'... mark and period'
Used to describe a piece (typically of Chinese porcelain) that bears the mark of a particular period, and was made in that period.

If you spot a bargain for sale at an online auction, and worry that others will spot it too, why not contact the seller? Email them to ask if they have a 'buy it now' fixed price. Don't be surprised if they don't, as it's likely that others have already made the same enquiry and the seller suspects they may have a treasure on their hands.

Don't forget to factor in the costs and logistics of shipping. If you live in London, shipping a table you bought in Dallas, Texas will add considerably to the purchase price, even if it's sent by ship.

Don't consider size alone, think about weight, too. Heavy metal or glass pieces can cost more than they are worth to send through the post. This consideration often keeps prices unusually low. It can also affect the general interest paid to an area by collectors for that reason.

Beware of buying items online that are made up of multiple pieces, even if the price looks temptingly low. Something like a Victorian dinner service is best bought in person, as if it needs to be sent through the post or a shipper, every single piece will need to be wrapped individually to avoid breakage.

Always use a secure online payment system to pay for your purchases. Never send your credit card details by email, and be wary of passing them on by telephone. Most dealers and sellers on online auction sites will use Paypal's secure systems.

Don't be upset if the item you bought on eBay or another online auction site doesn't arrive in a day, or even a few days. Most sellers are private individuals with full-time jobs and family life, with any selling being an irregular or even a one-off activity.

It's always worth emailing a dealer to ask for more information about an object, or if there is any flexibility on the price. You have no idea how long they may have had it for sale. Always ask for extra photographs, as you may spot something (good or bad) that they haven't.

Save your keyword searches of online auction sites as the site will often email you when an item related to it is listed. This enables you keep up to date with what's coming up for sale as it happens.

UP-AND-COMING TALENT

If you're collecting on a budget or have a gambler's eye for future investments, check out university and college degree shows. Only buy what you like and you won't be disappointed if the artist doesn't go on to become the new Damien Hirst or Tracey Emin. If they do, you've lucked out twice.

By buying art from degree shows, you'll be sure to have an unusual collection, and you'll be supporting the creators of tomorrow's art and antiques.

Always take away a maker's or designer's email address and if they have one, their website address. Check back frequently to see where they are having their next exhibition to keep up with their changing style.

It gets addictive, just like gambling, drugs or sex. It's like putting a coin in a slot machine. It might not pay off this time, so you put another quarter in and keep doing it until you are tapped out or finally hit the jackpot.

BRYAN PETRULIS, AUTOGRAPH COLLECTOR

SELLING

A piece may come up for sale because the collector
has fallen out of love with it, no longer has the space
for it, or wishes to refine a collection and free up funds
to buy something better. But some pieces can, and will,
never be sold. As collectors grow, they usually end up
selling more frequently, and the lines between being
a collector and a dealer can blur. The Canny Collector
never sells something without first knowing what it is
and what it's worth.

BE PREPARED

Your chosen method for selling an item will depend
on the time available to you and will range from doing
the whole thing yourself on an online auction site or at
an antiques fair, to selling a piece to a dealer or via an
auction. Simply put, the more you do, the more money
you will 'earn' from the deal. The more someone else
does, the more money they will earn.

The time taken to sell a piece includes time spent
developing levels of expertise in different skills from
photography to packing.
The Canny Collector uses the economic and financial
boom times to filter and refine their collection.

Consider the costs of various routes of sale before choosing
one. If your item is worth under £100/$150, it's unlikely that an
auction house will be very interested and, if they are, their fees
may wipe out much of what it makes.

Look out for art or items connected to a place. A
watercolour of the Lake District might make the most
money when sold in an auction or dealer's shop in the Lake
District. It's likely to make less money in Cornwall.

A DEALER'S LOT

If you gasp at the prices in top city-centre antique dealers' shops, and expect to sell for those prices yourself, rent or buy a shop nearby to really understand how it works. Such dealers work with an exclusive, wealthy and international client base who expect (and receive) the highest quality alongside exceptional levels of service.

Many people don't like selling to a dealer because they feel that their special piece becomes purely a traded commodity. Not so – most dealers are passionate people who invest time, love and attention, and their own cash into their stock.

If you're going to become a part or full time dealer, build up a look that is distinctly you, but is still commercial or, alternatively, specialise in an area. The market is stratifying and much of it is becoming more decorative in nature.

A dealer may offer you less than an auction house estimate, but bear in mind that you'll have to pay auction house fees and take the chance that it might not sell for the sum you want, or even sell at all. A dealer will usually pay their offer immediately. Alternatively, they may take the object on consignment, and pay you when it has sold.

A dealer's price tag may be anywhere from around 30–100 per cent more than the price they paid you. Shocked? Don't be. Dealers have overheads to cover, including stand or shop rent, utilities and business taxes.

SELLING

Have you ever wondered how much money a high-street
retailer makes on massively reduced sale prices?
Quite a lot usually. If they can still make money on a
discount of 50 per cent or more, consider how much
they make at full price. By comparison, the actual cost of
a good antique or collectable is often much more than
50 per cent of its retail price.

Like us, dealers have to make a living. You pay accountants
and plumbers for their expertise and experience, and the
same must be true for antiques dealers.

AUCTION KNOW-HOW

Don't be put off if auction houses, particularly in upper
tiers, ignore your objects. Sotheby's introduced auctions
of rock and pop memorabilia in 1981. Before then, the sale
of such objects at an auction house like Sotheby's would
have been unthinkable. Times change, and companies will
chase areas where there is money to be made.

Always listen to the auction house specialist's advice
when deciding on the level of an estimate and reserve,
particularly the price that an item won't be sold at less
than, known as the 'reserve'. Specialists have a firm grasp
of the market at the time of selling, and know how your
object is likely to perform in it via their services.

Always choose an auction house that lists its auctions on the
Internet as well as in a hardcopy catalogue. Better still, see
if the auction house illustrates all of the items and publishes
them on aggregator sites such as the-saleroom.com.

... you are asking me to sell members of my family.
(in response to a billion dollar offer for his collection.)

WALTER ANNENBERG, PUBLISHER & DIPLOMAT

Pay attention to the auctioneer's terms and conditions.
If your object sells for £500, fees will be deducted,
which may include anything from 10–25 per cent seller's
commission, a photography fee, an insurance fee and
maybe a handling or 'lotting' fee. Some auction houses
also charge for their services if the item does not sell.

Although auctions run throughout the year, the two
peak times for auctions are in spring and autumn. Some
jewellery, books, gentlemen's accessories and other
'gift' items can also sell well in December.

Underbidders are enormously important to sellers and
the auction house – the more the better. Don't feel as
if you've wasted their time if you don't win anything,
you've still helped the auction by participating.

Before the dawn of the digital age, high end and specialist
items would often only fetch the best prices in a few well-known
auction houses with global reputations. Now that most auction
houses have an international reach through their websites,
aggregator websites and search engines, the playing field has
become more even. When selling, the Canny Collector often
plays auction houses off against one another over vendor's
commission rates and services.

If an auction estimate is set at £400–600 (for example) the reserve
should be at the bottom end of the estimate, or below it. In
some parts of the world, the law defines this.

I don't like masterpieces having one-night stands in
collectors' homes between auctions.
(commenting on collectors 'flipping' his works for quick profits.)

ROBERT RAUSCHENBERG, ARTIST

SELLING ONLINE

Apart from a clear photograph, the most important part of any listing are the keywords. Online auction and fixed-price websites such as eBay.com, etsy.com and bonanza.com are mainly explored by using keyword searches. Ensure you mention any maker or designer name, what the item is, and the colour or size of the item.

Always make sure you list your item in the correct category. It's also often worth listing in more than one category. Some buyers search by keyword within categories.

If you're not sure in which category to place your item, how to describe it, or how to pitch it, browse or search through the most appropriate category to find similar pieces in the 'completed auctions' section of the site.

Don't use the word 'rare' unless it really is. It's misrepresentation and you'll irritate experienced bidders.

Start your eBay lot at 99p/99c. If the title contains the right keywords, a good description and plenty of useful photographs, it'll find its place in the market at that time and sell for the right price.

Fully pack, but don't seal a package containing an item to be sold online. Take it to the post office to obtain different quotes for shipping within your own country and abroad. That way you can examine the item if a bidder asks a question, while being sure that your quotes are accurate and keeping the object protected from damage.

Always include postage costs for other major countries in your listings. If you don't, obtain them and have them at hand as online auctions are a global forum and foreign buyers will ask. If you decide to limit your market to within your country, which is not recommended, make this absolutely clear.

Schedule the listing of your objects for sale according to when the listing will start and end. The Canny Collector starts a seven day listing on a Sunday evening. More people are at home and are able to browse and use the Internet. Not only will you maximize the exposure your item gets when it is newly listed, but more people will be able to bid on it in the all important last few minutes of an auction, potentially resulting in a higher price.

Bad times for selling include any holiday or vacation periods, such as summer or over Christmas. People are usually saving, or are away on holidays at this time. The first six weeks after New Year can also be a poor time to sell, as many people are waiting for their first pay–cheque and then cutting expenditure to pay for the expense of the festive period.

Don't panic and withdraw an object from an online auction if there are no bids, or the price remains low right up to the day when the auction ends. The time with the most bidding activity is usually the last hour of an auction. Sometimes nothing much happens until the last few seconds.

Once an item sells, get in touch with the buyer to arrange payment and delivery, and keep the buyer updated. This will help you gain important positive feedback.

Although it would cause the collector to 'spin in their grave', inherited collections passed on to descendants often end up being broken up in the saleroom or sold to various dealers.

VALUE

Don't own something just because you think it'll make you money in future, own it because you love it, and want it to enrich your life. The 'price' is what an object is offered or sold at, while the 'value' is what the object is worth to the buyer. One may be far higher than the other, and often they have very little to do with one another.

KEY INFLUENCES

Many think that the antiques and collectables market is staid, dusty, dry and unchanging. That couldn't be further from the truth. Although values don't change as quickly as price and can't be tracked over similar time periods, rises and falls can be just as dramatic.

The most dramatic effect on financial value is caused by changing fashions and tastes. Style mavens, interior designers, high street retailers, TV programmes and magazines all play a part. The fall in value of many traditional antiques is partly due to the success of a Swedish furniture store throughout the 1990s.

I maintain that the true worth of a collection cannot – and should not – be measured solely in terms of its monetary value ... the beauty an individual sees in an object and the pleasure and satisfaction he derives from possessing it cannot be accurately or even properly gauged exclusively in terms of dollars and cents.

J. PAUL GETTY, INDUSTRIALIST & ART COLLECTOR

Unlike stocks and shares, the cost of a transaction in the fine art and antiques worlds is large. Bear this in mind when buying or selling, as it impacts on the 'value' of a piece considerably. For example, an auction house can take a sum equivalent to around 45 per cent of the hammer price of a piece. This is made up of fees charged to the seller and the buyer, and is used to cover costs and continue the business.

When a market peaks in value, two key groups of collectors are lost. First are those who enjoy being proven right in their foresight. Second are a number of people who collected early on for a lower price. If the market has eye appeal, these people will be replaced by others, but this effect usually contributes to a plateau or drop in interest and pricing.

MAKING A PROFIT

Approach book prices taken from specialist price guides (such as those for stamps or die-cast models) with great caution. A figure given here is a guide for an item that is in absolutely the very best, or 'mint', condition. Unless a number of experienced collectors or independent experts agree that your piece is in that condition, work down from there – often some considerable way. Where relevant, any accompanying accessories, packaging or paperwork must also be complete, intact and in a similarly perfect condition.

Learn about different colourways and variations in size, detailing and accessories, as they can make all the difference to the value of a piece. This is of great importance with die-cast toys and some ceramic figurines, such as those by Royal Doulton.

The contents of an original package don't always increase the value. In most cases, it is more important that the packaging is intact and entirely original.

If it's the financial side of collecting that drives you, don't confuse speculation with investment. Buying at the right price and selling at the right time – when the market is peaking and the general financial and economic situation is healthy – is critical.

Selling a piece for more than you paid for it should be a complement to your taste and acumen, and a more important adjunct to the profit.

Some core markets never fall out of fashion. Examples include stamps and coins, whose general values have been retained over time, and in some cases increased at a time when prices being paid for most antiques have fallen. Items at the top end of a market or of the very finest quality are always desirable. The risks are high, however, so always buy wisely. That said, the returns can be impressive. Actor Hugh Grant bought an Andy Warhol painting of Elizabeth Taylor in 2001 for £2m and six years later he sold it for nearly £12m!

Don't disregard the value of collecting something to stop it from being forgotten. The financial value may be low, but it's no less worthwhile than a collection of silver.

I think there's so much in modern life that is transient. Antiques anchor us, give us a link to the past, but they also tell us a lot about our common history.

FIONA BRUCE, ANTIQUES ROADSHOW & BBC TV PRESENTER

Look out for forthcoming films about comic-book heroes and heroines. If a film proves to be a blockbuster, values for vintage memorabilia can rise as more people – many of them new to the character – are drawn to collecting. A good example of this are new films featuring characters such as Spider-Man or Transformers.

PROVENANCE

Provenance is important, and can increase the value of a piece. Look out for original stickers indicating that the piece is from a particular collection, or for a gallery label on the back of a picture. If the collection or gallery is important, or has direct links with the artist, this could increase the value. You may be able to research more of the history behind the piece. Provenance is critical for antiquities, as an item may be fake, stolen or illegally excavated and exported.

The Canny Collector will spot quality in a piece and acquire it, even if nothing is known about it, such as who designed and made it, and when or where. A little research and a lot of luck will reveal that information, but sometimes it will be years before the opportunity presents itself.

Ivory has become even more of an emotive subject than it ever has been in recent years. Nobody can excuse or forgive the deplorable slaughter of elephants, but is it right to destroy all antique ivory, including sculptures, chess sets, netsuke and inlaid furniture? Whatever your view, be aware of the legalities of buying and selling, and be prepared for increasing levels of criticism.

NOSTALGIA

Nostalgia is a key driver for collectors. Many people collect things that they were not allowed to have as children or, as is more often the case, that they loved as a child, but lost on reaching adulthood. Parents have a lot to answer for! As a result, the desks of many high calibre, senior executives of technology and other companies are littered with 'Transformers' and 'Star Wars' related memorabilia.

Collectors with an eye on future value should consider what today's younger generations may want to collect when they grow up. As generations of collectors age and start or stop collecting, entire markets change. For example, demand for prewar Dinky Toys is falling as those who remember them stop collecting, whilst values for 1950s–1960s Corgi Toys have been rising, because they appeal to the generation of collectors who are now most active. The same is true for characters. Whilst those who collect cowboy characters of the 1930s–1950s are falling in number, characters from The Simpsons, Toy Story, and other much–loved TV programmes and films may be the *next big thing* for many speculative collectors.

Some markets should be eternally popular. Star Wars, for example, has attracted collectors since the first toys were released in 1977. New films in later decades have created yet more collectors in different generations, and the trend now looks set to continue. It's unlikely that these films will ever fall from influence and relevance. Pay close attention to storylines and characters, as the toys and memorabilia related to them may have greater or lesser meanings for different generations.

As more of our aims in life become based on our experiences rather than study or possessions, will film, television, event and travel related memorabilia become the hot tickets of the future? It's much easier for many people today to relate to and enthuse over a poster from a rock concert, or a colourful vase bought on holiday in a French flea market than to an 18th-century porcelain tea bowl.

CONDITION

Condition is one of the most important factors to consider when buying or selling an object, along with the age and rarity and desirability of an object. It's not just about buying in the best condition possible, as some antiques and collectables shouldn't look 'new'.

SOUND ADVICE

Don't ignore damaged rarities. They can be a good way of adding a rare and expensive piece to your collection at a more affordable price. Many can sell for surprisingly high sums of money. A good example is Beswick's rare 'Duchess with Flowers'. In mint condition, values can be around £1,000, but even a broken one can fetch at least half that.

For nearly all limited editions, the condition and completeness of the box and any other packaging is critically important. It should be completely undamaged and in bright, original condition.

Having the original box makes a major difference to the value of an item. However, as this has been widely known for some years now, many people have kept the boxes for more contemporary items. As such, they make less of a difference to value.

ASSESSING CONDITION

Mint condition is the 'top of the tree' condition-wise and is the term used to describe something that is still in the original condition in which it left the factory. That means it will be unused and show no signs of wear. An alternative term used is 'new old stock', indicating that it was shop stock that was never used.

It's always better in the long run to own one object in truly mint condition, than it is to own a number of the same or similar objects in used or worn condition. The piece in mint condition will likely be scarcer and will always find a number of ready buyers.

Look with your fingers, as well as with your eyes. Run your fingers and fingernails around the edge of the rim of a ceramic or glass piece to feel any roughness, restoration, chips or flakes. Although it's tempting to ignore them as signs of wear commensurate with age, every tiny scratch or dent contributes towards the condition of a piece.

Always try to photograph any label on an antique or collectable. You never know, it might be the only one found so far with a label, and it could solve a mystery. The same goes for original boxes, which can reveal important information about the maker, date and any variations.

Smell inside a 1950s–70s Lucite plastic box handbag before buying it. If it smells of chemicals, walk away. The smell indicates plastic 'rot' which cannot be reversed. Examine the piece more closely, and you'll see a network of fine lines known as crazing, which indicate the same thing.

A crack in a bisque doll's head can reduce the value by as much as 70 per cent.

Whilst tears and losses on printed paper ephemera such as posters can often be repaired, if the damage –say surface scuffing or a tear – affects the image itself, it's considerably more detrimental to the overall condition and value.

Tap a vase or bowl with your finger – if it sounds dead and dull, it's cracked or restored somewhere, even if you can't see where immediately. If it rings like a bell, it's fine.

Restored areas of ceramic will often feel warm to the lips and cheeks, more so than the main body of the piece.

It's generally a very bad idea to repaint a die-cast or tinplate toy, even if it is chipped and worn. It'll only make it even less desirable to a collector.

Suitable restoration to a damaged piece can often cost more than the restored piece is worth. If it's precious to you, it's worth considering. If you're planning to sell it, get an estimate from a professional restorer first. Bear in mind that some collectors may prefer to restore something themselves, or may even prefer it in untouched condition.

Always consider proportion and shape, and check against photographs in books. Some shapes were prone to damage, for example elongated Art Nouveau 'Berluze' shape glass vases. Many were cut down and had their rims refinished following accidents.

If in doubt, don't clean off the grime of age until you've sought advice. It would be wrong to strip the surface off a worn and used 18th century snuff box, warmly coloured piece of 19th century mahogany furniture, or the petrol-like and grey 'bloom' from a coin, as these are sought-after features to collectors.

A collection makes its own demands. Many artists have been collectors. I think of it rather as an illness. I felt it was using up too much energy.

HOWARD HODGKIN, ARTIST

DINKY TOYS

150

ROLLS - ROYCE SILVER WRAITH

FAKES, REPRODUCTIONS and COPIES

The best way to avoid buying a fake or a reproduction is to build up specialist knowledge. It's not just about reading books and looking at pictures, as there's no replacement for handling as many objects as you can. There are also clear differences between fakes, reproductions and copies – for more information, see page 67.

Reproductions and fakes found in the marketplace today are not always new. For example, Georgian drinking glasses were widely imitated in the 1920s. The Victorian period is particularly renowned for reproductions and look-alike pieces due to an obsession with different historic styles. Some pieces of furniture were often made up using pieces from various older, period pieces of furniture.

HINTS AND TIPS

There is a market for fakes, copies and reproductions. Sometimes, perhaps owing to cost or rarity, they're the only option. Some are even worthy of study themselves. If a fake is identical to an original, and simply differs in who made it and where and when it was made, is it right to disregard it?

The old cliché, 'if it looks too good to be true, it probably is' most certainly applies to the world of antiques, vintage and collectables.

Many of the largest outdoor antiques fairs have reproduction tents or areas. It's always worth visiting them to see what is being reproduced at that moment, and to handle the reproductions so that you can familiarise yourself with them.

Many of the wisest dealers and collectors also buy the best fakes and reproductions. If they offer to walk you through their collection of fakes, jump at the chance.

Pay attention to size. Many reproductions are produced in moulds taken from originals. This process results in a reproduction that is slightly smaller than the original and that has less pronounced and defined details.

Weight is also important – many reproductions or fakes are lighter or heavier than originals for one reason or another, such as the use of different materials, or amounts of them.

When fakes and forgeries of pieces within a collecting area appear, it's a sign that the market has matured and 'arrived', as values and demand have risen enough to make the production of fakes and forgeries worthwhile.

As well as size and weight, consider colours, methods of manufacture and materials used when trying to identify fakes or reproductions. Handling as many authentic examples as possible will help you to discern the real from the reproduction swiftly.

FURNITURE

Furniture is often modified as fashions and domestic arrangements change, or as it passes from one generation to the next. Pieces are modified, cut down in size, legs are replaced, and decoration embellished. Consider proportion, look at the frame of a piece and check that all wood, veneer and details match.

You can often see if a piece of furniture is a 'marriage' of two different pieces by looking at the back – all backboards should match.

Truly original paint is extremely scarce. Furniture was painted so it could be refreshed for new fashions and generations over time. Most pieces on the market today have heavily restored, recent, or late 19th century at the earliest paint unless you're buying at the very top end.

Handles, locks and other drawer or door furniture are often replaced over time. Examine the front carefully and look on the inside to spot now redundant and filled holes.

Drawers can be useful in helping to date a piece of furniture from the way they are constructed. There are exceptions to the rule, however.

Early veneers were cut by hand and have a minimum thickness of 1.5 mm. Anything thinner is machine-cut and will date from the early 19th century and later.

Authentic inlay on antique furniture is often slightly raised from the surface of the piece, an effect caused by humidity that it is very hard to replicate.

GLASSWARE AND CERAMICS

As a rule, the bubbles that you find in glassware give no indication of age. In fact, most glass with internal bubbles dates from the 20th century.

Note how different ceramics factories indicate a second-quality piece. Many modify their mark, usually found on the base of an item. For example, Royal Doulton scratch a line through the printed mark on a piece, or drill a hole through the centre of it.

French company Samson and Cie (1845–1968) were well-known for producing imitations and copies of ceramics by famous companies such as Sèvres or Meissen. They were usually marked, but unscrupulous people have removed or modified these marks. Samson's ceramic material and glazes are usually different to originals.

Perhaps the most faked mark in the world of antiques is the famous Meissen 'crossed swords' mark, which was copied by many ceramics factories around Europe.

Always consider the quality of the material, design, proportion, detail, manufacture and decoration, which should all be of very high quality. If in doubt, compare it to examples in a good-quality reference book.

Fake Staffordshire pottery made recently in China is usually lighter in weight than originals and uses a granular bisque-like ceramic. Bases are also often bright and clean.

Chinese potters often copied the designs and reign or dynasty marks from earlier periods and applied them to their ceramics as a mark of respect and veneration, not as an intention to dupe or deceive.

SCULPTURE

Spelter statues and sculptures are lighter in weight than bronze versions. Scratch a small out-of-sight area and if a silvery metal is revealed, your statue is made from spelter. Spelter is quite brittle, so take care when moving it.

Look closely at Art Deco ivory and bronze statues. The ivory should have feint near-parallel lines and be well-carved, particularly on the fingers and face. The metal work should be softly patinated with age and cast smoothly and well. Fakes and reproductions have been made for decades, and usually use resin instead of ivory.

Modern brass is often very bright and yellow. By comparison, 18th and 19th century brass is more subtle, with deeper, softer and warmer tones.

PRECIOUS MATERIALS

Real amber floats in a solution of four teaspoons of salt in 230 ml (8 fl oz) of water. Fake amber sinks. Real amber feels warm to the touch, while glass amber feels cold.

Imitation ivory made from plastic (Ivorine) has lines similar to those found on ivory, but they are regularly placed and sized. There are no straight lines in nature.

Authentic jet builds up a static charge when rubbed on a carpet or woolly jumper – black glass does not. Black glass is also cold to the touch. Under a strong lens, you may even see striations and evidence of the rings of the tree that became real jet.

Authentic lignum vitae, one of the hardest and densest woods in the world, sinks in water.

TOYS AND COLLECTABLES

A teddy bear should have patches of wear in all the places a child's love would put them – the tummy, back, and maybe on the arms. If worn patches appear elsewhere, be suspicious. And take a long, deep sniff – nobody can fake the smell of decades of being a child's best friend.

Reproduction, novelty-shaped, cast-iron money banks usually have seams that do not fit together closely, a grainy cast finish, brash and bright paint, and often an unusually high rusty encrustation made with acid.

Beware of late 20th-century film posters bearing signatures from all the stars. How likely is it that they were all brought together to sign that many posters? Even if a poster is sold with a 'certificate of authenticity', find out who issued the certificate. Is it an independent industry body, or is it from the company selling the piece? Beware if it is the latter.

Collecting is a curious mania instantly understood by every other collector and almost incomprehensible to the uncontaminated.

LOUIS AUCHINCLOSS, NOVELIST AND LAWYER

WHAT IS IT EXACTLY?

There are major differences between fakes, reproductions and copies. And they're just the start. The meaning of the term used is all-important.

FAKE AND COUNTERFEIT
A fake or counterfeit is an object or work of art that has been produced, altered or modified to make it look better or older than it actually is. Counterfeit is usually used to describe fake money or documents.

FORGERY
A forgery is fraudulently produced to imitate something else. If a painting by a famous artist is produced by someone else in that artist's style and technique, using period materials, and bears the typical signature of that artist, it is a forgery.

COPY
A copy is an imitation of an original that does not pretend to be the original. It may even bear marks to show that it is a copy. If these marks are removed, and an attempt to make it closely resemble the original is made, then it becomes a forgery.

REPRODUCTION
This is used correctly to describe copies of pictures, prints or photographs made using photographic, mechanical or digital processes. It can also be applied to furniture and objects produced in imitation of earlier styles.

REPLICA
In its truest sense, a replica is a copy of something, often a picture, that was produced by the artist who produced the original. It has also been used to describe a (later) facsimile, copy or reproduction.

FACSIMILE
A direct copy of something, often used to describe printed signatures.

Some early 20th century German tinplate toys and 1950s–70s tinplate robots are being reproduced in China. Colours are usually different to the originals – often being too bright – and surfaces are shiny and glossy.

Fake scrimshawed teeth and tusks made from resin usually have flat bottoms with parallel lines where they have been ground flat on a machine. If there is an indentation, there's also no sign of the root. They will usually be heavier in weight, and the colour will be creamier and lacking the tonal variation seen on authentically inscribed real teeth or tusks.

Fake netsuke made from moulded resin will share many of the same characteristics as fake scrimshaw, and may also have inaccurately and inconsistently applied stains. Details will be poorly defined and the piece will feel rounded, not crisp, in the hand. If in doubt, heat a pin and gently stick it into the base. If it is resin, it will melt the resin and enter the base. If it is ivory, it will not.

TEXTILES

The pattern on a handmade rug can be seen on the back too. Go right down into the pile to find rows of knots. If they're not there, the rug was machine-made. The back of an old rug will appear almost shiny and knots will have been flattened. As you go into the pile look at the threads: they should appear darker in colour at the base and gently graduate up to a very light tone at the other end.

Consider colours and colour tones. The first synthetic aniline dye (mauvine) was introduced in 1856. Synthetic dyes are typically brighter and more vibrant than old organic dyes, which usually fade over time.

COMMON PITFALLS

The style of a mark, or the size and colour of a piece may indicate a different date to the suggested style of the design. For example, certain colours were introduced or became fashionable considerably earlier or later.

Many fakers inadvertently leave 'signature' or hallmark features or signs of a particular process in their work. Examining as many of the suspicious items as possible together, and then comparing them to originals, often reveals this.

Beware if something is in too good a condition for its age, particularly if it is a practical item. Tinglazed earthenware is very prone to chipping. If a piece purporting to be from the 18th century is undamaged and glossily smooth, be very suspicious!

Don't think that you can rest once you've identified something that makes an object a fake, forgery or fraudulent copy. The people behind it will know that you and others know, and will learn and adapt their production processes accordingly if there is money in it.

If something unusual or rare, or a particular type of object, appears too frequently suddenly, be suspicious.

The Victorian period (1837–1901) and Edwardian period (1901–10) saw many styles and design movements being revived. The Rococo style and Georgian furniture designs are good examples of this. Due to the industrial might of the UK, US and other countries at the time, a great many designs were mass-produced, even though they may look much earlier in date at first glance. Pay attention to elements of design, materials, methods of manufacture and makers' marks.

DISPLAY AND STORAGE

As your collection grows, it becomes an issue less about display, and more of storage. Enjoy your entire collection, fascinate and entertain houseguests, and remind yourself as to why you bought certain items by changing displays and revolving pieces in and out of storage.

DIVINE DISPLAYS

Objects often look best displayed in odd numbers, so in threes, fives and sevens, and so on. Vary the heights and sizes of pieces, and don't always put the smallest at the end or outside edge.

Use pedestals, perspex blocks or piles of antiquarian books to raise one or more pieces in a display.

Think in three dimensions and of depth and perspective. Don't just arrange pieces in a row, or place them closely together in a group. Play around with display options.

Even wildly different pieces can be linked together using a single motif or theme, such as colour or shape.

Space is as important as the objects. This is particularly true with pictures hung on a wall. Let things breathe.

Think about rhythm. Vary size and shape to add visual interest and drama. A collection of items of too similar size, shape or colour can often look dull.

Visit country houses and museums for inspiration. Historic methods of display can be updated or 'down-sized' well.

Geometric arrangements of objects hung on a wall will usually look stunning. Contrast straight lines, such as those of the wall itself, with curves to add drama.

Placing objects in front of mirrors, such as on a mantelpiece, allows all-round patterns to be viewed.

Glass comes to life when back-lit – for example, when placed in front of a window. The mood and tone of the piece changes in different lights, from the brightness of morning to the warmth of evening.

If you collect 'flat art' such as paintings, prints or drawings, add variety and depth to your collection by finding complementary sculpture. Alternatively add objects that pick out certain colours in key works.

Sometimes the clash and drama caused by displaying very different things together brings out qualities or similarities in both that you may not have seen before. The good proportions and clean lines of some good Georgian furniture work well in a Modernist interior, which can share the same core themes. Expressionist art can work well with early-19th-century, hand painted porcelain.

A room can be filled with innumerable things and yet have a perfect atmosphere of repose, if they are chosen with thought and care so as to form one harmonious background. The furniture should not stand out as a series of silhouettes, but merge into the background, the highlights being sufficient to show its form.

CHARLES PAGET WADE, ARCHITECT, POET AND COLLECTOR

It's not just about the objects. Use lighting to add drama and highlight key objects in your collection. Use a spotlight to highlight a single piece placed in an alcove or on an otherwise empty shelf.

The play of light, shadow and perspective given by candles and mirrors at night adds a sense of sparkle and fantasy to objects of any age.

Although it is currently seen as good taste to display objects against white or light, plain colours, consider what the objects would have been displayed against originally. Greek or Roman sculpture works against Pompeiian red, and an arts and crafts vase works well with William Morris wallpaper or fabric.

If you have high ceilings, don't be afraid of using the height available to you. Put large, dramatic objects or entire collections on top of furniture or hang pictures or mirrors above furniture.

Flip through high-end interiors magazines like
The World of Interiors for tips on how others have inventively combined living space with their collections Think of every part of the house as a potential display area, from the stairwell to the lavatory.
Surprise your guests!

Consider the choice of a frame as carefully as you did the choice of picture. A small picture needn't go into a small frame. Add drama with a deeper mount or discard a mount entirely and use a deep frame instead. Think three dimensionally.

Don't be afraid to experiment, and free another side of a picture. Traditional oil paintings from the 17th–19th centuries don't always need ornate gilt frames.

Don't rule out screwing pictures securely to the back of a door, especially if it is shut when you're inside the room.

If you're really pressed for space, hang pictures over book shelves from nails in the shelves. Books can make a successful backdrop, especially if the rest of the room is similarly crammed.

Never trim a print or document down to make it fit within a frame or mount. In particular, never trim an etching down to, or inside, its impressed 'plate mark'.

Away from the great names, late 19th century and early 20th century etchings from the 'etching revival' of that period are currently very affordable. I've been buying these for £5–30 since I was a schoolboy.
They look stunning framed simply and hung close together in large groups of different sizes and subjects.

Collections of framed pictures of different sizes, themes and ages in different styles of frame look striking displayed in overlapping groups on shelves.

I'm an anorak. I've always been an obsessive collector of things. Richard Briers collected stamps. I collect cars and guns, which are much more expensive, and much more difficult to store.

MICHAEL GAMBON, ACTOR

Over-sized single pictures needn't be hung at all and can be displayed on the floor, leaning against a wall.

Don't use a sprung-metal plate holder to display a plate on a wall, as it puts the plate under pressure and can damage it. Invest in proper display mounts.

Common themes in seemingly disparate objects can come together to cross the centuries.

Having said on a different page of this book that space is important and objects should be allowed to breathe, I can say that, for me, maximalism is the new minimalism. Gather it, group it, and gather and group more. There's fun, as well as safety, in numbers.

SAFE STORAGE

Every time an object is picked up or moved, it is at risk of damage. Choose a place to store an object where it can sit undisturbed. If you are stacking boxes or crates, be aware of their weight.

Stack pictures against a wall as vertically as possible, and ensure that only the frames are in contact with one another. Glass can break and pressure from a frame or picture wire loop can puncture or stretch a canvas. Cover the stack with a blanket to protect it from dust.

Always wrap items in acid-free tissue paper. Never use newspaper for storage. Bubblewrap with small bubbles is practical for ceramics and glass. Never skimp on either. Although it may seem expensive to buy, it's almost certainly less expensive than replacing or restoring the object it is protecting.

DISPLAY AND STORAGE

The ideal temperature for storing books is around
18–22 °C (65–75 °F), with a 50 per cent relative humidity.

A cool, well-ventilated room is essential for storing
books and paper ephemera. Leave a gap behind
books, between the wall and the books, to further aid
ventilation. Ensure books can't move but aren't too
tightly packed under pressure. Avoid sagging shelves,
as this puts pressure on the tops of the books.
Dust gently and regularly, away from the spine.

Don't hang pictures or textiles (even framed) directly
above radiators, table lamps or in strong light.

Bathrooms with regularly used showers or baths
can only be used to display objects that
won't be damaged by moisture.

The warmer the air is, the more moisture it can hold.
You should air rooms containing your collection regularly.

ENJOY IT

Don't be afraid of using a piece in your everyday life.
After all, it was originally made to be used. I think a
bottle of supermarket wine always tastes better when
drunk from a Georgian rummer, and I'm sure the
glassmaker would be happy that his glass is being used
nearly two centuries later. In many cases, you'll find
that an antique or vintage piece costs less and adds
more style than a similar brand new example.

*One cannot collect all the beautiful shells on the beach.
One can only collect a few, and they are more beautiful
if they are few.*

ANNE MORROW LINDERGH, AVIATOR AND AUTHOR

CARE AND REPAIR

Many objects suffer from the effects of age and use over the years. Accidents happen and collections must be kept clean. The Canny Collector knows what should and shouldn't be cleaned, and how to do it.

GENERAL ADVICE

Always seek professional advice before cleaning something if you feel uncomfortable about it. Never plug in antique or vintage electrical goods without first having them checked by a qualified electrician. Never rewire an item yourself, unless you are qualified.

Think before you clean. The lustrous result of years of wear, grime, polish and care, known as the 'patina', is an appealing feature to collectors, and its presence will reassure buyers and can increase the value.

Instead of dusting a piece, which often just pushes the dust elsewhere, consider using a vacuum cleaner. Place some muslin over the nozzle to reduce the suction and to prevent small or loose parts from disappearing up the tube.

If you're planning on buying an item to sell, ask yourself if the cleaning or restoration really needs to happen to maximise your profit. Many low- to mid-market dealers or collectors who sell won't restore or clean an item, preferring to leave that decision to the person to whom they sell it.

If you do break a piece and intend to have it repaired professionally, take extra time to find every single piece, no matter how tiny. Wrap each piece individually to avoid further damage.

FURNITURE

The cost of restoration – particularly reupholstering a piece of furniture – can often eat into, if not entirely gobble up the profits in a piece. Always consider this carefully. Your choice of reupholstery may not be someone else's cup of tea.

Don't be afraid to cover an antique or vintage chair in bold, modern fabric to refresh it and make it fit into your home. It can always be replaced.

Although it's often better to let wood speak for itself, don't be afraid to repaint or refinish a piece of antique furniture. If you're worried about how it will affect the value, ask an expert first. Provided you're not modifying something of importance or great value, with a little thought you'll breathe new life into a piece, and make it desirable again.

Consider antique painted furniture carefully before renovating it. Although it's unlikely to be the original paint, many collectors prefer aged, period paint.

Clean wooden furniture using a mixture made up of one cup of boiled linseed oil, two-thirds of a cup of turpentine and one-third of a cup of white vinegar.

To remove bad smells from inside furniture, try placing one of the following inside, before hoovering it out a few days later: cat litter; cotton balls soaked in pure vanilla and placed on a saucer; fresh, dry coffee ground; a bowl of baking soda mixed with an essential oil.

Never trust the handle alone when moving a box; always support the weight of the object itself too.

To remove candle wax, apply crushed ice in a plastic bag to make the wax brittle, then carefully flake it away with your fingernail. Buff furniture back up to a shine with polish.

To remove white water rings, use a specialist commercial product, a warm liquid mixture of 100 ml (4fl oz) olive oil and 30 g (1½oz) paraffin wax, or a mixture of white vinegar and potato flour. Apply each sparingly and leave on for a few hours. Remove the excess and repolish, if necessary, with tinted furniture polish.

Old ink stains are best left alone, as they'll add character to a piece. It's all part of the life story of the piece – just imagine what happened when the inkwell was knocked over. Was a passionate love letter being written, or did the lover arrive unexpectedly?

GLASS AND CERAMICS

If washing glass or ceramics in your sink, submerge a towel to line the bottom of the sink. It'll help protect your pieces from damage if you accidentally drop them.

Allow for a grubby glass vase bought at a winter car boot sale or flea market to warm up before plunging it into hot water to clean it. Otherwise you risk thermal shock cracking it.

Always care for your collection, as one day it may financially take care of you.

ANONYMOUS

To remove yellow or brown stains inside antique cups and saucers, paint on a thin layer of hydrogen peroxide (15 per cent content is ideal) and seal it in a bag for three days. Repeat until the stains have vanished. Don't use bleach. Always follow the health and safety instructions on the peroxide container.

Regular Coca Cola removes a huge range of grime and dirt from ceramics, glass and metalware but make sure you know what you're doing first.

Dry mirrors or glass after cleaning with scrumpled up newspaper to achieve a streak-free shine.

Don't soak bisque (unglazed porcelain) or some types of unglazed pottery, in water for long periods. Dab warm distilled water on, and dry quickly afterwards. Artists' paintbrushes of various hardnesses can be used to work water into crevices, and to remove dry dust deposits.

Car paint polish such as T-Cut makes a glass vase shiny and more resistant to finger marks from handling.

Free a stuck decanter stopper by dripping olive oil around the neck where the stopper enters the neck. Wait for a few hours until it has seeped inside and gently twist and remove it. Never force it.

METALWARE

Every time you clean silver, you remove a microscopically thin layer of the metal. This is because the grubbiness is actually oxidised silver – 'cleaning' silver simply removes it. Fine details and hallmarks can be polished away by too-frequent, over-zealous cleaning. Never use polish on 'blackened' niello silver decoration.

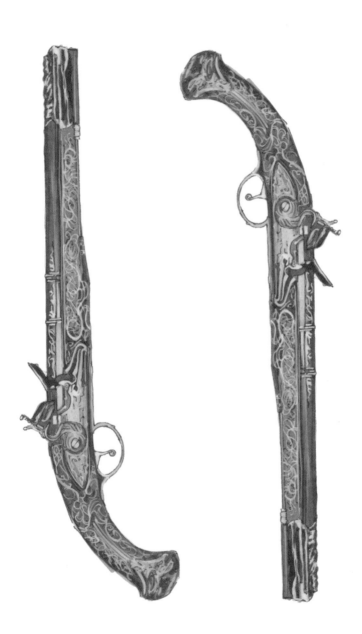

Don't store silver cutlery or similar pieces using elastic bands. They are best stored in airtight plastic bags to avoid tarnishing from hydrogen sulphide in the air.

If you use silver dip, don't completely immerse items with mechanical or moving parts, for example propelling pencils, as the dip may damage other metals in the mechanism.

To remove stains in aluminium vessels, gently boil freshly chopped rhubarb submerged in water. The acid should remove the stains after an hour or so.

Other than with proprietary cleaners, brass, copper and pewter can be cleaned using a paste made from mixing two teaspoons each of salt, vinegar and flour. Apply it, allow it to dry and wash off.

Pewter can be cleaned (if you must) by rubbing it with the leaves of a cabbage. Buff with a lint-free cloth after.

TEXTILES AND UPHOLSTERY

Beware cleaning any coloured textiles, fabrics or rugs made before the mid 19th century, as the coloured dyes are likely to be vegetable dyes and may wash out or run when wet. Test an unseen area, and seek advice if the colours run. Always use distilled water. Note the difference between grime and fading. Cleaning will never restore vibrancy to faded colours. Store paper and textile works in containers made of plastic. Any tissue paper used must be acid free.

Every passion borders on the chaotic, but the collector's passion borders on the chaos of memories.

WALTER BENJAMIN, PHILOSOPHER AND CRITIC

LIMITED EDITIONS

Be wary of limited editions, and check the quantity that was or will be produced. Always buy from as low an edition as possible – around 500 or fewer. If an edition runs to 50,000 items, be aware that more than 50,000 people must want one in the future for its value to rise. It's the old rule of supply and demand.

A limited edition of a collectable only runs to as many items as the manufacturer or maker thinks it can sell. Be aware that not all editions are completed. For example, only 24 out of a proposed 50 may have been produced. The Canny Collector discovers the reason for this and chooses whether or not to buy accordingly.

Note the difference between limited production and limited edition. Pieces in a limited edition are restricted to a set quantity, with each one being numbered individually (in most cases). It is usually impossible to know how many pieces are made in a limited production run, which is restricted by a time period only.

Always keep all the original paperwork and packing sold with a limited edition. Although the certificate is usually the most important part, other than the item itself, the box, accessories and even the internal packaging must also be present in order for it to fetch the highest prices.

Try not to unpack or use the object, even though this seems a great shame. For example, most modern limited edition fountain pens have never seen the light of day, as they are kept sealed in their boxes by collectors who are keen to preserve their 'investment'.

Once a limited edition has sold out, values can rise exponentially in a very short period of time. If you missed out, hold out, as this rise is typical and the vast majority of values fall back down again after the 'moment' has passed and collectors' interest moves on. Only a small percentage continue to be very valuable over a long time period.

To remove wine stains, dab the stain as quickly
as possible to soak up as much wine as you can.
Then sprinkle talcum powder or potato flour liberally
and remove when tacky. Repeat if neccessary.
Finally wash with glycerine and then water.

Shoe polish can be removed by wiping with a clean
cloth and a little white spirit. Use glycerine to remove
dried coffee stains. Afterwards, clean with water,
mop up any excess and allow to dry naturally.

If you think a book, teddy bear or soft toy is infested, seal
it in an airtight bag and leave in the freezer for a few weeks.

Although it may look dark brown and dirty, never, ever
clean a bronze sculpture or Asian work of art with metal
polish until it's bright and shiny. Removing this 'patina' will
reduce the value by well over half.

OTHER OBJECTS

Don't glue any paper objects such as stamps, postcards or
prints into albums or onto boards. Use mounts, which are
specially made for the job.

Clean jewellery using a cotton bud dipped in warm, soapy
water, or use a very soft brush to remove compacted,
ingrained grime.

Clean ivory and bone by dipping a freshly cut lemon slice
in salt and rubbing it gently on to the surface.
Rub in a little baby oil to restore the sheen.

Breathe new life into gilt frames using gilding wax,
applied with a finger or brush. For larger areas, seek
advice from an art supply shop about using gilding size
(glue) and gold powder. Take the frame with you
if possible so you can match up the colour of gold.
Gold coloured spray paint is rarely successful.

THE NITTY GRITTY

The devil is in the detail, and the difference between a colour, size, shape or detail, no matter how small, can be the difference between a desirable and valuable piece and trash. Not only that, but understanding the meaning behind a feature, even something as simple as the material, can allow the object to tell you something about it, such as its date. When you get down to the nitty gritty, the magic starts to happen.

When researching an area, buy everything you can that shares common features. This includes shape, colour, design elements and manufacturing process. When you have a mass of items, arrange them in rows matching up shape, colour and pattern. You'll soon weed out errors, and ranges will build up and be revealed.

FURNITURE

The three main woods used for furniture span three different periods. Oak was used up to c.1670, walnut from c.1670–1735 and mahogany from c.1735–1810. All were also used later. Exotic woods usually date from the 19th century onwards.

Radiograms are interesting and the cabinets can be very stylish and of high quality, but they are usually of little interest or value because it's hard to collect them owing to their size and the technology is uninteresting and out-dated.

The way furniture is constructed can tell you alot about its history. Take note of small details, like dovetail joints.

CERAMICS AND GLASS

The roughly circular 'broken' area on the bottom of
a glass piece is where the pontil rod was snapped
off when the item was made or finished by hand.
Sometimes this is ground away leaving a smooth or
polished concave disc or a completely flat base.

If glass is exactly the same thickness all around
the body, it's most likely to be machine made.

Tap a drinking glass with your fingernail, if it rings like
a bell it's lead crystal. If it doesn't, it's soda glass.

The way a piece was made and decorated can help to
date it. For example, transfer-printing was developed
in the early 1750s, so any transfer-printed pattern dates
from after then. Colour printing was developed in the
late 1830s and popularised during the 1840s, so colour
printed items are from this date and beyond.

Most glass made before the 20th century is unmarked,
and is identified from the design and methods of
manufacture. The rise of the designer and of brand
marketing led to the introduction of labels and, to a
lesser degree, marks from the 1930s on.

Pay attention to a label's material – paper usually dates
from the mid 19th century onwards, foil from the 1920s
onwards and plastic from the 1960s onwards.

*I hold that few human activities provide an individual
with a greater sense of personal gratification than the
assembling of a collection of art objects that appeal to
him and that he feels have true and lasting beauty.*

J. PAUL GETTY, INDUSTRIALIST AND ART COLLECTOR

To tell the difference between transfer-printed and hand-painted patterns, look closely. If you can see tiny dots and an even surface, the item is almost certainly transfer-printed or screen-printed. If you can see brush marks, and even perhaps feel them with your fingers, then the piece is probably hand-painted. Many ceramics made twenty years before and after 1900 were decorated with a combination of both.

Earthenware and stoneware (pottery) is opaque and usually a brown, buff colour. It is typically covered with another glaze, such as opaque white, or coloured, tin glazes.

Porcelain, which is typically translucent, can be divided into two categories. Hard paste (true) porcelain is very white and can be crisply and finely modelled. It almost looks like icing on a cake, and glazes are thin and glassy. Soft-paste porcelain ranges from white to grey in tone, is more brittle and has a grainier texture.

A fine network of cracks running through a glaze, known as crazing, is not necessarily a bad sign. It cannot be restored.

Numbers that are impressed on the base of ceramics usually indicate the shape number. Painted numbers may indicate the pattern number, or even the batch, customer or order number. They may also relate to the decorator, who would have been paid a sum of money for each piece decorated.

Details in marks can pay dividends, and help to date a piece. For example, American pottery Rookwood added a flame to their mark each year after 1886, ending in 1901, when there were 14 flames in total and the pottery moved on to roman numerals.

Royal Worcester, Sèvres, and Wedgwood also used certain marks for dates.

Pay attention not only to the style, but also to the colour of the mark on the base of a ceramic as this can indicate an earlier or scarcer piece. For example, Beswick Beatrix Potter figurines are usually worth more with earlier gold marks than later brown marks.

To fetch the highest prices – apart from rare patterns such as 'Sunray' – Clarice Cliff and Art Deco ceramics should combine an Art Deco pattern with vivid colours and an Art Deco shape.

If you're looking for something visually stunning and large, chargers offer a lot of bang for your buck in terms of pattern. Clarice Cliff's Art Deco patterns are desirable and expensive; some patterns by Charlotte Rhead or Enoch Boulton are potentially undervalued.

Look out for storage jars with unusual labels, such as 'Meal' on Cornishware. These are likely to be rare and collectors will vie to add an example to their collection.

Learn about production dates, as this information can pay off. Although the Royal Doulton figurine of 'Top O' The Hill' was designed in 1937, it has been in constant production since then. Figurines designed at the same time, but that were not produced after the war, will be considerably rarer and are usually worth much more.

Recently I've been buying Star Wars figures again. When I was a kid, I couldn't afford them. Now I can so I've been buying them and keeping them in their box for a later date when they'll be worth a lot of money.

MACKENZIE CROOK, ACTOR

SILVER, GOLD AND JEWELLERY

Look closely at hallmarks, those that read 'E.P.N.S.' indicate the piece is 'Electro Plated Nickel Silver', so it is silver-plated and made from the 1840s onwards. It is not 'English Pure Natural Silver'.

It's well worth learning about the marks used in other countries to denote silver and gold. These can vary from the word 'STERLING' in the US to numbers to all manner of different motifs – all of them tiny. Such information might enable you to spot something someone else has missed at a fair or auction. Similarly, familiarise yourself with marks that denote silver-plated and gold-plated items, such as 'Rolled Gold' which does not indicate solid gold.

Two to four digit numbers stamped on the base of metalware such as pewter teapots, rarely indicate the date. They're more likely to indicate the shape or model number.

Consider the setting of a piece of costume jewellery. Invisible settings, developed by jeweller van Clef & Arpels look exactly as the description suggests. Prong settings use thin wire 'claws' to hold the stone in and allow light up through it to give it sparkle. Less expensive pieces have stones glued into recesses in the metal backing.

PRINTED MATTER

First editions are from the first print run of the first edition of a book, which is nearly always a hardback. To identify a first edition, look for the number '1' in the series of numbers on the copyright page. Some publishers state that a book is a first edition, while others use a sequence of letters. Always check that the publishing date and copyright date match and check the original publishing date online. Book-club first editions tend to be ignored by most collectors. Interest in first-edition paperbacks is growing, but values tend not to be as high as for hardbacks.

To reach the highest values, a book must have its dust jacket, if it was issued with one. Both the dust jacket and the book must be in excellent condition.

The back of a picture can often yield a lot of information. Look for gallery labels, auction lot stickers, inventory numbers and any other marks. Also consider the type of label, font and any designs used that may help with dating.

To date photographs or pictures to a period, look at the styles of clothing and hair. But don't just rely on that, make sure all the other factors add up, too.

Look out for rerelease posters, or English language foreign film posters, as these are often much more affordable than their British or American counterparts, while retaining a strong flavour of the film. A good example is the rerelease of Casablanca in 1956 which costs a fraction of the £25,000 plus needed to buy an original!

Look out for unusual, decorative and suitably saucy postcards. Whether it's an Edwardian card showing a village fete or disastrous event, a card with an embossed and coloured Art Nouveau design or a Donald McGill seaside design, it will nearly always be worth more than a card showing a church that looks much the same now as it did then.

To date advertising or packaging, consider its design and the social habits and desires of the day. Take particular note of any lettering and the colours used. The material from which it is made, and the way in which it has been printed will also help.

MEMORABILIA AND COLLECTABLES

A photograph of an early 20th century teddy bear with its original owner can double the value of the bear.

In terms of quantity and size of production, Royal memorabilia peaked around the Diamond Jubilee of Queen Victoria (1897) and declined thereafter. Her Diamond Jubilee saw Britain's ceramics powerhouses at their strongest, the distribution network across the Empire at its best, and the largest audience with the means and desire to buy memorabilia.

Although he abdicated before his coronation, royal memorabilia for Edward VIII, later the Duke of Windsor, is not generally as rare or valuable as one might think (even though there are valuable pieces). Factories went into overdrive producing memorabilia many months before a coronation or royal event, and still do.

If you didn't make a ticketed event like a football match or rock concert, don't throw the ticket away out of disappointment. If the event turns out to be important or even legendary, your unredeemed (and rare) ticket could be worth a lot to a collector.

Don't disregard a broken or incomplete object. Instead consider it from a salvage perspective. For example, a vintage fountain pen lacking its gold nib can still yield other parts that a collector or restorer may pay for, particularly if they are in a rare colour or pattern.

Although planes by Stanley or Norris are often sought-after, the most desirable and valuable tools, will be those rare examples that were finely made for special techniques, such as making musical instruments.

If buying character collectables such as animation cels, look for imagery where the character is clearly seen and doing something that is closely associated with their character.

Don't ignore memorabilia related to Christmas, Halloween and Easter dating from the 1920s–1960s. This genre has a huge following in the US, where it's known as 'holiday memorabilia'.

Tinplate toys were hand-painted until around 1900, when transfer-printing took over. This technique was used into the 1970s, and is still used for reproductions. To date a piece, look for maker's marks and consider the form. Zeppelins were popular from 1920–1937, and robots and spacecraft became popular in the 1950s. Toys with 'mystery action' will date from the 1950s on.

Pay attention to the livery on British railway memorabilia. If it is for the LNER, GWR, SR or LMS, it will date from 1923–48. If it is for British Rail, it dates from after 1948.

The form of an antique ivory or wooden chess set will identify its type, and may even help to date it.

Often used as a derogatory term by many traditionalists, 'novelty forms' can be desirable and valuable as novelty adds appeal. Barware, gentlemen's accessories, pepperettes and other small items are good examples.

HISTORIC AND CELEBRITY COLLECTORS

History is littered with collectors who are preserving history. Due to the rise of the Internet and an increasing interest in modern and contemporary design from the 20th and 21st centuries, it is said that collecting art and antiques is dying. I'd argue that this has been said many times before throughout history, but collecting objects from the past (however old) has never died. Like everything, it simply goes through cycles of popularity, but always endures. Here's a list of some important collectors from history, which proves that, despite the many changes social, economic and technological developments and evolution throw at us, collecting has always been with us. As long as the wealthy, powerful and influential continue to collect, so will the rest of us. I've added a notable fact about each collector's collection to give you something to aim for. It also shows that, as a collector, you're in good company!

• Gaius Verres (c.120 BC to c.43 BC) abused his position as governor of Sicily to build a vast art collection, much of it plundered from temples and private houses. He even built a special ship to take his spoils to Rome.
• Jean, Duc de Berry (1340–1416), who commissioned the *Très Riches Heures* Book of Hours which was begun in 1412 and completed in 1489.
• Archduke Ferdinand II (1529–1595), whose collection of tapestries, armour and paintings forms much of the Kunsthistorisches Museum, Vienna.
• King Charles I (1600–49), who spent £28,000 in 1627 on works by Mantegna, Titian and Caravaggio from the famed Gonzaga collection.
• Sir Hans Sloane (1660–1753), whose collection of over 71,000 objects was bequethed to the nation to form the British Museum.
• Frederick Augustus I (1670–1733) was so obsessed with Oriental porcelain that he swapped an entire regiment of dragoons for a series of vases, and brought about the discovery of the secret of making porcelain in Europe.
• The Duchess of Portland (1715–85), after whom the famous Roman glass 'Portland Vase' is named, and whose vast collection of 'shells, ores, fossils, birds' eggs and natural history' took around 50 days to sell by auction according to fellow collector Horace Walpole.

- Charles Willson Peale (1741–1827) opened his private museum in Philadelphia in 1802 which, until it closed in 1827, contained thousands of exhibits from the world of nature, including a five-headed cow.
- Sir John Soane (1753–1837), whose collection includes Hogarth's *The Rakes Progress*, paintings by Canaletto and Turner, 5,887 Greek, Roman and Egyptian antiquities, and Pharoah Seti I's alabaster sarcophagus.
- John Pierrepont Morgan (1837–1913), who bought entire collections intact, and also owned Catherine The Great's snuff box, Napoleon's watch and some of Leonardo da Vinci's notebooks.
- Baron Ferdinand de Rothschild (1839–1898) built Waddesdon Manor to house his vast collection. Since then, his family have donated over 50,000 works of art to public institutions, including rare Renaissance pieces.
- Andrew Mellon (1855–1937) who spent $6,654,033 in 1931 on 21 paintings from the Hermitage, which went on to form the basis of the National Gallery of Art in Washington, D.C.
- Sigmund Freud (1856–1939), who believed that all collecting is related to the loss experienced when we first learn to use the toilet, also spent much of his life building a collection of Greek and Roman antiquities.

Collecting on a lavish scale is not restricted to historic personalities, however. Here's a list of today's celebrity collectors and what they collect.

- Andrew Lloyd-Webber: Victorian paintings and art.
- Brad Pitt: Arts and Crafts and Bauhaus objects, and Tiffany lamps.
- Demi Moore: Dolls (she has reputedly even built a house for them).
- Elton John: Photographs, spectacles and so much more!
- Johnny Depp: Insects and rare books.
- Leonardo di Caprio: Vintage posters and dinosaur skeletons.
- Nicholas Cage and Jonathan Ross: Comic books.
- Quentin Tarantino: Board games and vinyl records.
- Rowan Atkinson and Jay Leno: Classic cars.
- Sarah Michelle Gellar and Kelsey Grammer: First-edition and rare books.
- Tom Hanks: Vintage typewriters.
- Whoopi Goldberg: Books and Bakelite and plastic jewellery.
- The late Queen Mother: Wemyss pottery.

TYPES OF COLLECTORS

As collectors, we tend to go through a number of stages.
First we amass items; second, we identify a type or range
to focus on, third we aim to complete it. Once that's done,
or once the chase becomes too hard or too expensive,
we often start to collect something else.

You might recognise yourself as a combination of any
two or more of the types that follow, or you might fall
neatly into a single category: every collector is different.

Collections reveal a lot about their owners, how they
see themselves, and the way they want to be seen.

How do you tell the difference between the novice and
expert collector? The novice looks for the signature
first, while the expert notices it last.

THE COMPLETIST
The collector who simply has to have it all. Once an
area is identified, the boundaries are marked out
and everything within them is a must-have.

THE CABINET COLLECTOR
This collector loves to fill a cabinet, or fill a hole
in a cabinet if he or she gives something away or sells
something. Until another cabinet is acquired!

THE COLLECTION COLLECTOR
For this collector, none of their chosen subjects seem
to quench their thirst for long. He or she holds on
to them for memories' sake, while moving on to
something else. They feel unable to part from any of
their previous collections, however. If this collector
can't collect, there's a hole in their life.

THE BURNOUT COLLECTOR

The collector who buys something like a Lalique wine glass for £100, then comes back to buy another to make a pair. He or she loves the pair, so comes back and buys a Lalique bowl for £400. They love the way it looks and works with the glasses, so come back and buy a vase for £5,000. Then they're too scared to return for a few years, or are never seen again.

THE NASCENT DEALER

A collector who buys because it's a good deal and to make money, rather than through a desire to own a piece. He or she usually ends up either dealing around a day job, or doing it full time.

THE BABY BOOMER

Born from the mid–1940s to the mid–1960s, these collectors used the wealth they accumulated through employment to build large and typically focused collections once their children had grown up. They often focused on traditional areas such as porcelain and 18th and 19th century furniture.

THE MILLENNIAL COLLECTOR

Otherwise known as Generation Y, born from the late 1970s–2000s, they don't see themselves as collectors. Instead, they use vintage and antique items, which become part of their lifestyles, from fashion to kitchenware. Three of the same object are often too many. It's about the look and experience, not the learning.

THE SPECULATOR

These collectors buy purely because they believe that something will rise in value and return a sizeable profit – either because they have read something or because someone has convinced them of this fact.

THE COMPETITIVE COLLECTOR

There's a little of this collector in all of us. We want
the biggest, the smallest, the most detailed, the best,
the rarest, or whatever. This is often also one
manifestation of a display of wealth or learning,
or a desire to show taste or move up the social ladder.

THE CUSTODIAN

Although other factors play a role, these largely
altruistic collectors collect to preserve pieces from the
past for future generations because they believe them
to be of historical, social or economical relevance or
importance. Advanced custodians may write books
or publish websites on the subject.

THE CONTROL FREAK

Highly organised and structured, this collector may
have stamps carefully sorted into albums, or entire
'lives' contained in dolls' houses. It's their way of
dealing with unpredictable and uncontrollable real life.

THE NOSTALGIC

Many people collect because it reminds them
of childhood, or enjoyable events in their past.
They collect memories and the objects are the
vessels that carry them – the keys to
open them in the mind's eye.

THE DECORATOR

This collector amasses a wide variety of objects
that often have no intrinsic value. However, when arranged
or displayed by the collector who is naturally skilled at
such things, they are transformed, and transform the room
around them. They bounce off each other, creating an
energy, look and feel, and imbue the room and viewer
with their spirit and essence.

THE ACCUMULATOR
These collectors are in the early stages of collecting. The bug has just bitten them and they enthusiastically seek out and hoard everything related to their new love, regardless of quality or condition. Canny Collectors usually develop and grow out of this type.

THE HOARDER
The hoarder's collection grows vast and varied, disorganised and without focus, logic or theme. Nothing is sold, given away or even thrown away. There is usually a lack of self-control and strategy.

THE HUNTER GATHERER
It's the thrill of the chase that counts the most here. Driven by a primal need to go out and bring things back, the activity is as much, if not more, fun than the objects themselves. There's often no focus to a collection, and objects are quickly replaced in the collector's affections by whatever the next 'kill' is.

THE 'IMPORTANT' COLLECTOR
Obsessed and obsessive, these extreme collectors encourage a collection to become the most important part of who they are. They believe that the collection imparts and has immense social, economic and even historical importance.

There are two types of collector, I think. There are those who are quite academic and get into the archaeology of finding the earliest example of a particular idea. Then there are those interested in what's new.

ADAM CLAYTON, BASSIST, U2

A-Z of Antiques & Collectables, edited by Judith Miller, Dorling Kindersley, 2008

A Passion for Collecting, Caroline Clifton-Mogg, Jacqui Small, 2002

Antiques Detective, Judith Miller, Dorling Kindersley, 2007

Antiques & Collectables Fact Book, Judith Miller, Miller's, 2008

The Antiques Magpie: A Fascinating Compendium of Absorbing History, Stories, Facts and Anecdotes from the World of Antiques, Marc Allum, Icon Books, 2013

Antique Trader Guide to Fakes & Reproductions, Mark Chervenka, Antique Trader, 2007

The Arcanum, Janet Gleeson, Bantam Books, 1999

The Art of the Steal: Inside the Sotheby's–Christie's Auction House Scandal, Christopher Mason, Putnam, 2004

Care & Repair of Antiques & Collectables, Judith Miller, Miller's, 2008

Christie's Guide to Collecting, edited by Robert Cumming, Phaidon & Christie's, 1984

Collecting & Display, Alistair McAlpine & Cathy Giangrande, Conran Octopus, 1998

Confessions of a Collector, Hunter Davies, Quercus, 2009

Confessions of a Poor Collector, Eugene M. Schwartz, Edition Taube, 2012

Cracking Antiques, Mark Hill & Kathryn Rayward, Mitchell Beazley, 2010

Decorative Arts, Judith Miller, Dorling Kindersley, 2006

The Elements of Style: An Encyclopedia of Domestic Architectural Detail, Stephen Calloway, Firefly, 2005

Encyclopedia of British Pottery and Porcelain Marks, Geoffrey Godden, Barrie & Jenkins, 1987

Fake, Forgery, Lies & eBay: Confessions of an Internet Con Artist, Kenneth Walton, Weidenfeld & Nicolson, 2006

In Flagrante Collecto, Marilynn Gelfman Karp, Abrams, 2006

Framed: America's Art Dealer to the Stars Tells All, Tod Volpe, ECW Press, 2003

The Grammar of Ornament, Owen Jones, A & C Black, 2008

Glass: A to Z, David J. Shotwell, Krause, 2002

The Greatest Collecting Tips in the World, Tracy Martin, The Greatest in the World, 2008.

How to Make Money Out of Antiques, Judith Miller, Miller's, 1995

Is it Genuine? How to Collect Antiques With Confidence, John Bly, Miller's, 2002

Journal of a Collector, Alistair McAlpine, Pavilion, Books Ltd 1994

The Joys of Collecting, J. Paul Getty, Hawthorn Books, 1965 & 2011.

Killer Stuff and Tons of Money, Maureen Stanton, Penguin, 2011

London Goldsmiths 1697–1837 : Their Marks & Lives, Arthur Grimwade, Faber & Faber, 1990 (Also covers silver)

Men and Collections, Brian Jenner, New Holland, 2003

Miller's Antiques Encyclopedia, edited by Judith Miller, Miller's, 2013

Miller's Antiques Marks, Judith Miller, Miller's 2013

Miller's Antiques Price Guide, Judith Miller, published bi-annually, by Miller's

Miller's Collectables Handbook, Mark Hill & Judith Miller, published bi-annually by Miller's

Objects of Desire: Design & Society Since 1750, Adrian Forty, Thames & Hudson, 1986

The Penguin Dictionary of Decorative Arts, John Fleming & Hugh Honour, Penguin, 1989

Sleuth: The Amazing Quest for Lost Art Treasures, Philip Mould, Harper Collins, 2009

Sotheby's: Bidding for Class, Robert Lacey, Little, Brown & Company, 1998

Tips, Tools & Techniques, Georgia Kemp Caraway, University of North Texas Press, 2012

GENERAL INFORMATION AND PRICE GUIDES

antiques.about.com
millersantiquesguide.com
worthpoint.com

NEWSPAPERS, MAGAZINES AND ONLINE LISTINGS

antique-collecting.co.uk (UK)
antiquexplorer.com (UK)
antiquesnews.co.uk
antiquestradegazette.com (UK trade newspaper)
antiqueweek.com
apollo-magazine.com
drouot.com
homesandantiques.com (UK)
maineantiquesdigest.com (US trade newspaper)
midcenturymagazine.co.uk
themagazineantiques.com (US)
vintagexplorer.co.uk (UK)

INTERNATIONAL TRADE ORGANISATIONS

American Society of Appraisers - appraisers.org
Antique Dealer's Association of America - adadealers.com
Antiquarian Book Dealers' Association - aba.org.uk
Antiquities, International Assoc. of Dealers of - aiad.org.uk
Appraisers' Association of America - appraisersassoc.org
Australian Antique Dealers' Association - aada.org.au
Belgian Association of Antiques & Art Dealers -
antiques-chamber.be
British Antique Dealers' Association - bada.org
Canadian Antique Dealers' Association - cadainfo.com
Czech Association of Antiques Dealers - asociace.com
Danish Art & Antiques Dealers' Assoc. - dkau.dk
Dutch Association - kvhok.nl
French Auctioneers' Association - symev.org
French National Antiques Dealers' Assoc. - sna-france.com
German Antiques & Art Dealers' Assoc. - bdka.de

Greek Association of Antiques Dealers - antiques.com.gr
International Federation of Dealer Assocs - cinoa.org
Irish Antiques Dealers' Association - iada.ie
Italian Antiques Dealers' Association - antiquariditalia.it
Italian Federation of Art Dealers - fimantiquari.it
London & Provinces Art & Antique Dealers - lapada.org
The National Antique & Art Dealers' Association of
America Inc. - naadaa.org
National Association of Valuers & Auctioneers (UK) - nava.org
National Auctioneers' Association (US) - auctioneers.org
New Zealand Antiques Dealers' Association - nzada.org.nz
Norwegian Antiques Dealers' Association - nkaf.no
Polish Art & Antiques Dealers' Assoc. - antykwariusze.pl
Portuguese Assocation of Antiques Dealer's - apa.pt
Posters, Internation Assoc. of Dealers - ivpda.com
Society of Fine Art Auctioneers (UK) - sofaa.org
Spanish Antiques Dealers' Association -
federacionespanoladeanticuarios.com
South African Antiques Dealers' Association - saada.co.sa
Swedish Art & Antiques Dealers - konstantik.se
Swiss Art Dealers' Association - khvs.ch
Tribal Art Dealers' Association - atada.org
Tribal Art Society - tribalartsociety.com

LIVE ONLINE BIDDING AND AUCTION CATALOGUES
artfact.com
auction.fr
drouot.com
icollector.com
liveauctioneers.com
the-saleroom.com

DEALER AGGREGATORS
1stdibs.com
antiques.co.uk
antiquesaregreen.org

decorativecollective.com
goantiques.com
onlinegalleries.com
rubylane.com
salvo.co.uk (architectural reclamation and salvage)
sellingantiques.co.uk
tias.com

MESSAGEBOARDS, FORUMS AND BLOGS
20th Century Ceramics & Glass - potteryandglass.forumandco.com
20th Century Design - 20thcenturyforum.com
Coins - coincommunity.com
Collectors Weekly - collectorsweekly.com
Glass Messageboard - glassmessages.com
Harry Rinker - harryrinker.com
Mark Hill (the author) - markhill.net
Obsessionistas - obsessionistas.com
Wristwatches - wristwatchforums.proboards.com

SPECIFIC SUBJECTS
20th Century Design & Designers - designaddict.com
Bakelite & Plastics - plastiquarian.com
Ceramics Marks - porcelainmarksandmore.com
Postwar Czech Glass - webareal.cz/ceskoslovenskesklo
Fashion (Vintage) - vintagefashionguild.org
Finnish Glass Design - designlasi.com
Glass Encyclopedia - glassencyclopedia.com
Inuit Art - katilvik.com
Oriental Porcelain - gotheborg.com
Polish Film Posters - cinemaposter.com
Roseville Pottery - roseville-pottery.net
Silver & Silverplate Marks - 925-1000.com
Silverplate Marks - silvercollection.it
Staffordshire Potteries - thepotteries.org
Stamps - stanleygibbons.com
Studio Potters & Potteries (UK) - studiopottery.com

GENERAL RESEARCH AND MORE
Antiques Diva - antiquesdiva.com (Antiques tours)
Antiques Roadshow (US) - pbs.org/wgbh/roadshow
Antiques Roadshow (UK) - bbc.co.uk/programmes/b006mj2y
Art Loss Register - artloss.com
European Patent Office - epo.org/searching.html
UK National Archives - nationalarchives.gov.uk
US Patent Office - uspto.gov
VADS - Onlive Visual Arts Resource - vads.ac.uk
Value My Stuff - valuemystuff.com

ACKNOWLEDGEMENTS
I must thank Anna Southgate for her editing skills and for her helpful suggestions about, and steely organisation of, my (very) raw text. Once again Ali Scrivens proved to be a solid (and patient) rock when it came to design. Mike and Debby Moir have given useful and thought-provoking tips amidst stimulating conversation over many a dinner after antiques fairs in Birmingham and London. I must also thank Philip Reicherstorfer for once again putting up with me while I researched, wrote and pulled together this book. As you can probably tell by now, it's based on the things I'm most commonly asked about. I've learnt a lot from everyone I've been lucky enough to meet over the past 19 years in this amazing industry, but I must thank Alexander Crum Ewing, Judith Miller and Graham Cooley in particular. There's so much more to see and learn, and I can't wait!